The Student Leadership Competencies Guidebook

The Student Leadership Competencies Guidebook

Designing Intentional Leadership
Learning and Development

Corey Seemiller

A Wiley Brand

Published by Jossey-Bass
A Wiley Brand
One Montgomery Street, Suite 1200, San Francisco, CA 94104-4594—www.josseybass.com/
higher education

Jossey-Bass books and products are available through most bookstores. To contact Jossey-Bass
directly call our Customer Care Department within the U.S. at 800-956-7739, outside the U.S. at
317-572-3986, or fax 317-572-4002.

Wiley publishes in a variety of print and electronic formats and by print-on-demand. Some
material included with standard print versions of this book may not be included in e-books or in
print-on-demand. If this book refers to media such as a CD or DVD that is not included in the
version you purchased, you may download this material at http://booksupport.wiley.com. For
more information about Wiley products, visit www.wiley.com.

Library of Congress Cataloging-in-Publication Data has been applied for and is on file
with the Library of Congress.

ISBN 978-1-118-72047-9 (paper), ISBN 978-1-118-79104-2 (ebk.), 978-1-118-79114-1 (ebk)

FIRST EDITION

PB Printing   10 9 8 7 6 5 4 3 2 1

The Jossey-Bass Higher and
Adult Education Series

Contents

The Jossey-Bass Student Leadership Competencies Database can be accessed at www.josseybass.com/go/studentleadershipcompetencies

Acknowledgments

THE STUDENT LEADERSHIP Competencies (SLCs) journey has been just that—a journey. It started with our wanting to create some evaluations for our leadership programs and turned into an amazing experience that has affected me significantly as a professional. I reflect on the early days in 2008 with my colleague, Tom Murray, and me making lists of leadership competencies that we thought might be good for us to focus on within our programs, and the wonderful guidance of Susan Komives in her suggestion that we look at the intersection of these competencies with academic learning outcomes. Since then, Tom and I spent years analyzing, evaluating, and coding what appeared to be endless amounts of data. As we learned over time how valuable that data was to both our practice and the field, we found creative ways to use it and share it.

By the time 2013 came around, it was time to code again. What we did as a team from 2008 to 2011, I did on my own in 2013 because Tom has since transitioned to new endeavors. I must say that I am quite familiar with just about every accrediting body in higher education and have spent much beloved time with their documents. But, although this part of my journey was mostly solo, I could not have even embarked upon it if it were not for the support of a few key people. First, I thank my partner, Karrie, for supporting my long days and late nights of coding on weekends and evenings when I'm sure she would have preferred that I ran errands or cleaned the house. She also put up with my continuous traveling and requests for her feedback as she sat through yet another round of my sharing my upcoming presentation with her. In context, the SLCs were born before my four-year-old daughter was. After her birth, time was more precious, and Karrie's support became even more vital. She always does whatever it takes to make sure I get to explore this exciting opportunity. And, of course, the support of my daughter, Kacey, has been great. She continues to ask whether there will be pictures in my book and often pretends she is working on her own book to be just like Mommy.

Next, I thank Tina Wesanen-Neil, my trusted colleague and friend, who has been nothing but supportive in this process. She has read, reread, and reread my writing. She has helped me brainstorm names for the competencies. And, she has helped me to implement the SLCs so that I truly could see how they benefit our programs.

I also thank Ebtisam El-Sharkawy, the assessment student assistant in our Leadership Programs office at The University of Arizona. Ebtisam has been instrumental in collecting data on our programs for the past two years, creating spreadsheet after spreadsheet to analyze the data, and then providing me with ideas and feedback on how to improve the measurements and the data collection and analysis process. During the 2013 coding round, she helped me gather many of the new accreditation documents and made my coding process easier.

Countless friends and colleagues have been incredibly supportive of me over the years and shared my enthusiasm for the Student Leadership Competencies. These individuals have assisted me in many ways, whether that has been through copresenting at conferences, giving shout-outs to the competencies in their presentations or writings, offering me opportunities to share my work, and providing continued support both publicly and privately. These supporters include many, but three key individuals have been Rich Whitney, Craig Slack, and Susan Komives.

Finally, I thank Erin Null from Jossey-Bass, who has worked tirelessly for several years to make this project happen. I thank her for her determination and continued belief in the importance of this work.

About the Author

COREY SEEMILLER RECEIVED her PhD in higher education from The University of Arizona and has worked with a variety of leadership programs in higher education, K–12, and in the community since 1995. She serves as the director of Leadership Programs at The University of Arizona, overseeing nearly nine thousand participants per year in ten curricular and cocurricular leadership programs, including the Arizona Blue Chip Program, the National Collegiate Leadership Conference, forty-five courses for credit in leadership, and the Minor in Leadership Studies & Practice. Corey teaches courses on foundations of leadership, global leadership, organizational leadership, critical perspectives on leadership, leadership strategies, social justice leadership, leadership for social change, and the capstone course for the Minor in Leadership Studies and Practice at The University of Arizona. She has taught other courses, such as multicultural leadership, critical thinking and decision making, and making career choices, at other higher education institutions and maintains an adjunct faculty role at Pima Community College teaching dynamics of leadership. Corey is cofounder and president of the Sonoran Center for Leadership Development, a nonprofit leadership center in southern Arizona that provides low-cost leadership development programs for community and educational groups. She has served as a facilitator with the YWCA Racial Justice Program, Anytown and Anytown, Jr. camps, ACUI's We-Lead, and LeaderShape. She is one of the creators of the Power, Privilege, and Oppression (P2O) social justice activity and travels nationally to facilitate P2O at institutions of higher education. Corey is a member of the International Leadership Association and the National Clearinghouse for Leadership Programs and has conducted research, presented, and published on leadership nationally and internationally.

Introduction

WHAT DO STUDENTS need to know, believe, be able to do, and engage in to be effective leaders in college, in their careers, and in society? *The Student Leadership Competencies Guidebook* and resources have been designed to provide tools for using leadership competencies in program development, curriculum design, and assessment to help students develop and enhance critical competencies to effectively engage in leadership.

What Are Competencies?

Competencies are knowledge, values, abilities, and behaviors that help an individual contribute to or successfully engage in a role or task. *Knowledge* includes information that is helpful for one to know in order to engage in an intended behavior. This may include understanding models, theories, practices, processes, and/or steps. *Values* are those attitudes or beliefs that one possesses that indicate that something is important. For instance, knowing how to make an ethical decision is helpful, but if one does not believe that being ethical is critical, then that may affect one's ethical behavior. *Ability* refers to one's skill level or motivation to effectively engage in a behavior. Some competency areas are about skill development, and practicing can help one enhance those competencies. Some competency areas are less about skill, though, so it is vital to consider motivation as a catalyst or barrier to one's ability to engage in a particular behavior. Finally, *behavior* is the engagement in the competency in an effective manner. Is one truly effective when engaging in the competency?

Why Focus on Leadership Competencies?

To adequately prepare students for their future careers, it is imperative to understand the competencies that are deemed necessary for effectiveness in their career roles. Knowing this can help provide a framework within which to design experiences that help college students better prepare for and develop essential leadership competencies specifically linked to their career fields. Because the use of competencies is commonplace in many professional organizations (Ammons-Stephens, Cole, Jenkins-Gibbs, Riehle, & Weare, 2009) and in nearly 75 percent of businesses (Conger & Ready, 2004), focusing on competency development in college will allow students to become familiar with the process and language of competencies prior to entering their career fields. Students will know what competencies will be expected of them in their future careers and can both intentionally develop the competencies necessary for their fields as well as articulate that development using competency language with prospective employers in the job search process.

Also, using competencies is an inherently intentional process. By identifying competencies before designing a program, then creating curriculum around those competencies, and finally measuring student learning and development, there is a process of intentional development at work. In an era of accountability, being intentional about student learning and development and then quantifying it through assessment is vital. Using measurable competencies is yet another vehicle with which to demonstrate effectiveness of leadership education and accountability in higher education.

How Were the Student Leadership Competencies Developed?

The initial list that would become the Student Leadership Competencies was developed in 2008 from an examination of the components inherent in the Relational Leadership Model (Komives, Lucas, & McMahon, 2013), the Social Change Model of Leadership (Astin et al., 1996), and the Five Practices of Exemplary Leadership (Kouzes & Posner, 2008), along with the standards outlined for leadership programs in the 2006 edition of the Council for the Advancement of Standards (CAS) in Higher Education (Dean, 2006) and outcomes from the ACPA/NASPA 2004 document, *Learning Reconsidered* (Day et al., 2004). A master list of all concepts, standards, components, elements, and competencies listed in these documents was created. In many cases, a concept like Vision or Empowerment appeared across multiple models or documents. In other cases, a concept only appeared once, like Evaluation. Some overarching concepts such as Critical Thinking appeared. Because critical thinking is a cluster of several competencies, it was vital to identify each of the specific competencies associated with critical thinking, such as Research, Evaluation, and Analysis.

After the initial list of competencies was created, the process of using this information to analyze learning outcomes from academic programs began. The first step was to research the programmatic accrediting organizations accredited or endorsed by the Council for Higher Education Accreditation, the U.S. Department of Education, and the Association of Specialized and Professional Accreditors. These three agencies serve as clearinghouses for programmatic accrediting organizations and in 2008 collectively housed seventy-two programmatic accrediting organizations such as AAMFT (American Association of Marriage and Family Therapy) and NASM (National Association of Schools of Music). Each programmatic accrediting organization accredits specific academic programs. An *academic program* is defined as a specific discipline and degree level, for example, a bachelor's in accounting or a master's in electrical engineering. Some programmatic accrediting organizations accredit only one academic program, whereas some accredit more than fifty. In total, in 2008, the seventy-two programmatic accrediting organizations accredited 475 undergraduate and graduate academic programs in the United States.

Once the 475 academic programs were identified, a master database was created to list the learning outcomes specific to each academic program. Some programs listed only one outcome whereas others listed several hundred. These learning outcomes included all knowledge, values, abilities, and behaviors expected of graduates of each academic program in order to be effectively prepared for entry-level work in the careers associated with that academic program.

Once the learning outcomes were identified for each of the 475 academic programs, the process of analysis and coding began. The initial list of competencies that would eventually become the Student Leadership Competencies was then compared to the learning outcomes for each academic program. Through this process of analysis, any learning outcome from an academic program that included a competency from the list was coded and matched with the appropriate competency. Not only did this process validate the initial list of competencies, other competencies could be added to the list based on emergent data from the learning outcomes analyzed. For instance, two of the competency areas added through emergent data were Confidence and Excellence. Although these were embedded in the literature used to create the initial competency list, they appeared less prominent than other competencies that were selected for the list and were not deemed as vital to being included. The continued prevalence of these competencies within the academic program learning outcomes validated the need to include these competencies after all.

This process resulted in the creation of the Student Leadership Competencies as well as a robust dataset that linked learning outcomes with applicable competencies. From this dataset, it was possible to determine the prevalence and frequency of each of the competencies within and across academic programs. In addition, data could be disaggregated by degree level and similar academic programs to better understand competencies necessary for different students in different contexts. The original findings of the 2008 dataset were published in the *Journal of Leadership Studies* in 2013 (Seemiller & Murray).

In 2013, the study was again completed by examining the updated learning outcomes of all original academic programs and adding new programs that had emerged since 2008. The total number of academic programs analyzed was 522. Given the emergent data, the Student Leadership Competencies list was again updated to reflect the new findings, and a new dataset was developed. In total for the 2013 analysis, nearly eighteen thousand learning outcomes were analyzed and coded.

In addition, the components and elements associated with the Relational Leadership Model (Komives et al., 2013), the Social Change Model of Leadership (Astin et al., 1996), Five Practices of Exemplary Leadership (Kouzes & Posner, 2008), Emotionally Intelligent Leadership (Shankman & Allen, 2008), and CAS Standards (Dean, 2006) have been cross-listed with the Student Leadership Competencies. This provides a resource to those using these models to easily incorporate the Student Leadership Competencies into a programmatic or curricular framework based on one or more of these models.

What Are the Student Leadership Competencies?

The Student Leadership Competencies consist of sixty competency areas within eight categories.

Each of the sixty competency areas includes four competencies that reflect each of the following dimensions:

1. *Knowledge (K):* Knowledge of or understanding of the value of a competency

   - Do I know how to effectively execute the behavior related to this competency?

2. *Value (V):* Value placed on a competency

   - Do I believe this competency is important?

3. *Ability (A) (Motivation or Skill):* Internal motivation to engage in a certain behavior or the skill level to perform a certain behavior

Category	Competency Areas	
Learning and Reasoning	Research	Synthesis
	Other Perspectives	Evaluation
	Reflection and Application	Idea Generation
	Systems Thinking	Problem Solving
	Analysis	Decision Making
Self-Awareness and Development	Self-Understanding	Scope of Competence
	Personal Values	Receiving Feedback
	Personal Contributions	Self-Development
Interpersonal Interaction	Productive Relationships	Others' Contributions
	Appropriate Interaction	Empowerment
	Helping Others	Providing Feedback
	Empathy	Supervision
	Mentoring	Collaboration
	Motivation	
Group Dynamics	Organizational Behavior	Group Development
	Power Dynamics	Creating Change
Civic Responsibility	Diversity	Social Justice
	Others' Circumstances	Social Responsibility
	Inclusion	Service
Communication	Verbal Communication	Facilitation
	Nonverbal Communication	Conflict Negotiation
	Listening	Advocating for a Point of
	Writing	View
Strategic Planning	Mission	Plan
	Vision	Organization
	Goals	
Personal Behavior	Initiative	Responding to Ambiguity
	Functioning Independently	Responding to Change
	Follow-Through	Resiliency
	Responsibility for Personal	Positive Attitude
	Behavior	Confidence
	Ethics	Excellence

- Do I have the ability, either the motivation within myself or the skill I need, to be able to effectively execute the behavior related to this competency?

4. *Behavior (B):* Engagement in a certain behavior

- Do I effectively engage in this competency when an appropriate situation arises?

Tenets of the Student Leadership Competencies

Following are the tenets of the Student Leadership Competencies. These tenets have guided the development of the competencies and provide a basis of understanding so that they can be utilized in the most effective and appropriate manner.

Foundation

- The Student Leadership Competencies were created using data from U.S.-based organizations; thus it is important to understand the cultural context within which the competencies exist.

- Although the Student Leadership Competencies highlight individual leader development, they can also be used to develop and evaluate group leadership.

Developing Competencies

- Although competencies can be learned, prior possession of specific traits may influence the depth, speed, ease, and effectiveness in acquiring and using a particular competency. For instance, someone who is more extroverted may approach developing the competencies related to Collaboration differently than might a person who is more introverted.

- Competencies are not the only form of development and evaluation that can be used to help students develop their leadership capacities. They are only one of many approaches and can be used simultaneously with other methods of development and evaluation.

- Unlike some competency models used in a business setting, the Student Leadership Competencies do not provide a mathematical formula for hiring, firing, and promotion and should not be used for selection or placement of students into programs or roles based on competencies they already have developed. In the higher education context, the Student Leadership Competencies are designed to be developmental, so that students can learn and hone their competencies in the college setting to prepare them for the future.

Using Competencies

- The Student Leadership Competencies are a toolbox. It is not necessarily a goal to have all students develop all competencies. The focus should be on developing the competencies that a student may need to use more frequently or more effectively than others.

- Leadership situations can be complex and contextual and call for the use of many competencies simultaneously.

- Being able to leverage competencies other individuals have that the student does not have can be valuable for the group process and outcome.

Competencies and Learning Outcomes

Learning outcomes refers to what students are expected to do or demonstrate at the completion of a learning experience, the end result of their learning. Programs have learning outcomes, courses have learning outcomes, and even many leadership roles have learning outcomes. So, what competencies do students need to possess and/or engage in to reach the intended learning outcome?

To answer this question, it is important to determine what competencies might be most helpful to a student in achieving a particular outcome. If, for instance, the desired outcome for a student is to be better at time management, perhaps developing the knowledge and ability dimensions of Evaluation, Organization, Plan, and Follow-Through might be useful. What if the student already has a great plan but struggles with completing it? Perhaps the focus would be only on the ability and behavior of Follow-Through. Maybe the student is great at time management in groups but is challenged in working alone. Then, perhaps it might be best to develop the knowledge and ability competencies of Functioning Independently. To achieve a learning outcome, a student may need only to develop and utilize one competency, whereas for other

---

FIGURE I.1

How Competencies Contribute to Outcomes

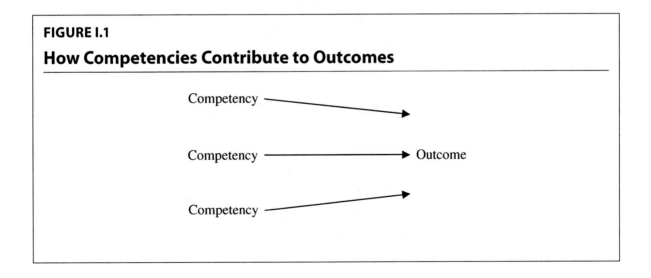

outcomes, the development and use of many competencies collectively may be necessary.

Using the Student Leadership Competencies

The Student Leadership Competencies Guidebook and resources can be used in both curricular and co-curricular programs at the college level for program design, curriculum development, and assessment. There are three resources to assist in this process:

1. *The Student Leadership Competencies Guidebook*
2. *Jossey-Bass Student Leadership Competencies Database*
3. *Self-Evaluation Templates*

Student Leadership Competencies Guidebook

The Student Leadership Competencies Guidebook is organized into chapters based on competency area. Each chapter begins with a description of how the competencies discussed in that chapter are important to leadership. This is followed by a vignette related to college student leadership that showcases the competencies in action. Each chapter is then divided into five sections: Competencies, Related Competency Areas, CAS (Council for the Advancement of Standards) Translation, Leadership Model Translation, and Curricular Ideas.

Competencies

The four competencies derived from each competency area are defined using the following dimensions.

1. *Knowledge (K):* Knowledge of or understanding of the value of a competency
2. *Value (V):* Value placed on a competency
3. *Ability (A) (Motivation or Skill):* Internal motivation to engage in a certain behavior or skill level to perform a certain behavior
4. *Behavior (B):* Engagement in a certain behavior

Related Competency Areas

Related competency areas are listed so that there is an understanding of how developing one competency may also intentionally or unintentionally develop another.

CAS Domain Translation

Each competency area can be translated to and from the domains of the CAS Standards and are listed in the *Jossey-Bass Student Leadership Competencies Database* as well as within each chapter in the book.

Leadership Model Translation

Each competency area can also be translated to and from existing leadership models. These are searchable in the *Jossey-Bass Student Leadership Competencies Database* but are also listed in each chapter of the book.

1. Relational Leadership Model

2. Social Change Model of Leadership

3. Five Practices of Exemplary Leadership

4. Emotionally Intelligent Leadership

Curricular Ideas

Although it is not a comprehensive or exhaustive list of curriculum, the ideas in these tables provide tangible ways to help students develop each competency. By using some of these curricular ideas, students may develop other competencies as listed.

Jossey-Bass Student Leadership Competencies Database

The *Jossey-Bass Student Leadership Competencies Database* can be found at www.josseybass.com/go/studentleadershipcompetencies and can be searched by Career, Competency, or Model.

Career

Each academic program has its own list of necessary leadership competencies based on the learning outcomes set forth by the programmatic accrediting organization. To find the list of competencies for a particular academic program:

1. Select a career field (for example, Business).

2. Then, select an academic discipline (for example, Accounting).

3. Finally, select the degree level (for example, Bachelor's).

This will populate with competencies for that particular academic program (for example, bachelor's in accounting).

Competency

The database can also be used to find models and career fields associated with up to five competencies at a time. To use this search function:

1. Select up to five competencies.

2. Then, select to search by either models or careers.

If the search is conducted by models, this will populate with the selected competencies and any corresponding components of each leadership model. If the search is conducted by careers, this will populate with the selected competencies and any associated academic programs.

Model

Many leadership programs use a leadership model as a framework for program design and/or curriculum development to ensure a well-rounded student learning experience. To find competencies based on a particular leadership model:

1. Select a model.

This will populate with the competencies associated with that model.

Self-Evaluation Templates

The *Self-Evaluation Templates* provide a concise means to evaluate each dimension of the sixty competency areas. They are based on the definitions of each of the competencies in the *Student Leadership Competencies Guidebook* and are not exhaustive evaluation measures, only brief one-item statements for students to use to self-report their perceived development. The following explains how to evaluate the competencies.

Evaluating Competencies

1. Open a blank word processing document. Add any questions or fields that you would like to gather information about, such as demographics or program feedback. This will serve as your evaluation form. If you have an existing evaluation form, you can simply follow the next instructions to add any competency self-evaluation templates.

2. Select the competency you would like to evaluate, keeping in mind the four dimensions. Will students learn about, value, develop an ability, or engage in [ethics, verbal communication, organization, and so on]? You can always select more than one competency dimension to evaluate.

3. The self-evaluation statements for the four dimensions of each competency area are listed in one *Self-Evaluation Template* file. For example, all self-evaluation statements associated with the four dimensions of Ethics are listed in the *Self-Evaluation Template* file for Ethics.

4. Cut and paste each self-evaluation statement you would like to include from the *Self-Evaluation Template* file to your evaluation form.

5. Repeat this process for all competencies you wish to evaluate across all applicable *Self-Evaluation Template* files.

Don't forget . . .

- If you are evaluating more than one competency, you can put them all onto one evaluation form.

- Make sure you fill in the blank space in the directions with the name of your program/course/event/experience/role.

- If you are building an online evaluation, you can offer the choices (Did not increase, Slightly increased, Moderately increased, and Greatly increased; or I did not, I did to some extent, and I did) in a drop-down menu or as radio buttons. Use a format that works best for your students.

Analyzing Competencies

In associating numerical values to responses, you can calculate averages for each self-evaluation statement as well as percentage of responses for each category. To calculate findings quantitatively, simply associate the following responses with the following numerical values:

Knowledge, Value, Ability

- Did not increase: 0
- Slightly increased: 1
- Moderately increased: 2
- Greatly increased: 3

Behavior

- I did not: 0
- I did to some extent: 1
- I did: 2

Evaluation Example: Quantitative Self-Evaluation Measurements

Please place an X in the box that most accurately indicates your level of competency development as a result of participating in the [program/course/event/experience/role].

	Did Not Increase	Slightly Increased	Moderately Increased	Greatly Increased
My understanding of the process of group development.				
The value I place on social justice.				
The skills I need to engage in inclusive behavior.				

Please place an X in the box that most accurately indicates your level of engagement in the following competency during your participation in the [program/course/event/experience/role].

	I Did Not	I Did to Some Extent	I Did
Consider perspectives other than my own.			

Using the Student Leadership Competencies: At-a-Glance

Following is a step-by-step process for using the Student Leadership Competencies and resources. This process can be done for programs, curriculum, courses, position descriptions, or any other curricular or design component related to student leadership development.

Evaluation Example: Quantitative Pre-Learning Self-Evaluation

In addition, to delve deeper into students' responses, you may want to include a measurement for each competency that explains particular responses. This would work best in online evaluations in which the tool you are using to build the evaluation allows this measurement to only appear for answers of "Did not increase" and "Slightly increased" or "I did not."

If you indicated that your competency development regarding [competency] did not increase or slightly increased as a result of participating in this [program/course/event/experience/role], please select the response that best explains why.

I have already developed this competency to the extent it was offered for this [program/course/event/experience/role].

The [program/course/event/experience/role] did not address or minimally addressed this competency.

The [program/course/event/experience/role] did address this competency, but I was not engaged or involved to the extent that I could have been.

Other_____

If you indicated that you did not engage in [competency] during this [program/course/event/experience/role], please select the response that best explains why.

There was no or very limited opportunity to engage in this competency during this [program/course/event/experience/role].

Although there was opportunity to do so, I chose not to engage in this competency during this [program/course/event/experience/role].

Other_____

Evaluation Example: Qualitative Self-Evaluation Measurements

After all of the quantitative measurements, you may also want to include measurements that elicit an open-ended response.

What was your most significant learning experience during_____?

How do you plan to apply this learning in your life?

I Am Developing a New Program				I Have an Existing Program
↓				↓
Consider your program and/or institutional values, goals, and needs in determining appropriate competencies.	→	Refer to the *Student Leadership Competencies Guidebook* for a description of each competency and select applicable competencies.	←	Match existing learning outcomes with competencies.
Is this program based on a leadership model? If yes:	→	Add appropriate competencies from the *Jossey-Bass Student Leadership Competencies Database*.	←	Do you want to include additional competencies based on a leadership model? If yes:
Is this program targeted toward students in a specific academic program? If yes:	→	Add appropriate competencies from the *Jossey-Bass Student Leadership Competencies Database*.	←	Do you want to include additional competencies targeted toward a specific academic audience? If yes:
Develop curriculum based on selected competencies. Do you need ideas for curriculum? If yes:	→	Refer to *The Student Leadership Competencies Guidebook* for curricular ideas for each competency.	←	Ensure the existing curriculum is appropriate to develop the intended competencies. Also, develop curriculum for any newly added competencies. Do you need ideas for curriculum? If yes:
Create evaluations of competencies you intend to measure.	→	Download the *Self-Evaluation Template* file of each competency area to find the appropriate competency self-evaluation statement you intend to use. Then, consolidate all measurements you have selected into one evaluation.	←	Create evaluations of competencies you intend to measure.

Chapter 1

Learning and Reasoning

Research

Leaders can often get inundated with the vast amount of information being produced and shared in a variety of formats, some of which is useful and some that is extraneous to the leaders' needs. It is important that leaders can produce and distinguish useful, legitimate information that is most applicable to each leadership situation.

Samantha is a member of student government, which is currently working with the institution's administration on the concern of student fee increases. She has been asked to provide research that backs the student government's position to keep fees low. To fulfill this task, Samantha gathers the most recently published schedules of student tuition and fees from peer institutions as well as researches scholarly articles documenting the detrimental effects of rising education costs. She uses this information to create a report to provide to the administration on behalf of student government.

Research Competencies
Understands how to research information effectively (Knowledge):
Understanding effective strategies to use when engaging in research, including understanding what constitutes legitimate research, knowing resources available to use when researching, and understanding how to navigate through the vast array of information to effectively find the necessary information.

Values researching information effectively (Value):
Believing that the best information is derived from using effective research strategies; valuing not just gathering any information, but the best information.

Has skills to research information effectively (Ability):

Being able to research information effectively by being able to determine what constitutes legitimate research, effectively utilizing available resources when researching, and being able to navigate through the vast array of information to effectively find the necessary information.

Researches information effectively (Behavior):

Using effective research strategies to not just gather any information, but the best information.

Related Competency Areas

- Analysis
- Evaluation

CAS Domain Translation

- Knowledge Acquisition, Integration, Construction, and Application

Leadership Model Translation

- Relational Leadership Model: Purposeful

Research Curricular Ideas

Dimension(s)	Curriculum	Other Competency Areas Developed
Knowledge	Offer a workshop covering tools and strategies for researching information effectively.	
Value	Have students discuss potential consequences of not using legitimate sources or not assessing for bias when doing research.	
Ability	Give students a topic to research so they can practice effective researching; have them share their research process; and then give feedback on their research skills.	Receiving Feedback
Behavior	Have students engage in a research project using only legitimate research and/or sources.	
Behavior	Have students critique a piece that is self-published by an individual.	Evaluation
Behavior	Have students research the same topic using a variety of sources and discuss the differences in information found among the sources.	Analysis

Research Curricular Ideas

Dimension(s)	Curriculum	Other Competency Areas Developed
Behavior	Have students prepare for and engage in a debate in which they do not know the argument they will have to make ahead of time, requiring them to research multiple perspectives.	Verbal Communication Advocating for a Point of View
Behavior	Give students a topic to research and have them compete with each other to see who can come up with the best (most comprehensive, legitimate, and so on) research related to the topic the fastest.	Evaluation

Other Perspectives

Leaders do not have all the answers. Thus, it is essential that they are able to truly consider other opinions, experiences, and outlooks to help them develop better solutions and approaches when dealing with leadership situations. Not only can this lead to better outcomes, but considering other perspectives helps leaders relate to and appreciate others more by better understanding their viewpoints.

Hilary, the president of her student organization, has been getting frustrated at the lack of attendance at the weekly meetings. Hilary wonders why with such a large membership that there has been such a low meeting turnout. One member, Mario, approaches Hilary after the meeting one day to let her know that as a general member of the organization he believed that the meetings were not engaging as they might be, because they mostly consisted of hearing Hilary talk. Hilary had never thought of that before because she was so engaged. Mario offers a suggestion to Hilary to have everyone break up into their committees at the meeting so as to be more engaged. Hilary thinks that is a great idea and restructures the format of the meeting to be more engaging of the general members. After restructuring the format, meeting attendance and engagement increased.

Other Perspectives Competencies
Understands the value of considering perspectives other than own (Knowledge):
Understanding how valuable considering perspectives other than one's own can be in terms of understanding and appreciating others, finding

solutions to problems by looking from another's point of view, and learning new information that may shape, confirm, or alter one's worldview.

Values considering perspectives other than own (Value):

Believing that considering perspectives other than one's own can be helpful in understanding and appreciating others, finding solutions to problems by looking at them from another's point of view, and learning new information that may shape, confirm, or alter one's worldview; believing that everyone can learn something from everyone else.

Motivated to consider perspectives other than own (Ability):

Being motivated to consider other perspectives by listening to others, considering their viewpoints in decision making, as well as not passing judgment on ideas one does not agree with; being open to different opinions and ideas.

Considers perspectives other than own (Behavior):

Considering perspectives other than one's own and allowing new information, differing opinions, and others' experiences to impress upon one's thinking and understanding and appreciation of others.

Related Competency Areas

- Problem Solving
- Receiving Feedback
- Empathy
- Others' Circumstances
- Listening

CAS Domain Translation

- Knowledge Acquisition, Integration, Construction, and Application

Leadership Model Translation

- Relational Leadership Model: Inclusive
- Social Change Model of Leadership: Controversy with Civility
- Emotionally Intelligent Leadership: Capitalizing on Difference
- Five Practices of Exemplary Leadership: Challenge the Process; Model the Way

Other Perspectives Curricular Ideas

Dimension(s)	Curriculum	Other Competency Areas Developed
Knowledge	Have students brainstorm the value that multiple perspectives can have on a decision.	
Knowledge	Have students research a current social issue in which there are a variety of conflicting perspectives; have them discuss how each of these perspectives has influenced the issue.	Research
Value	Have students journal about or discuss with others a time that they changed their opinion on an issue based on being exposed to another perspective.	
Ability	Select a leadership case study; have students come up with three different approaches to the same case study.	Analysis Problem Solving
Behavior	Hold an intergroup dialogue to encourage students to share their perspectives and experiences related to their social identities.	Others' Circumstances Verbal Communication Listening
Behavior	Have students discuss controversial topics and share their opinions with each other.	Verbal Communication Listening Advocating for a Point of View
Behavior	Have students research an issue and write about or discuss opposing viewpoints related to this issue.	Research

Reflection and Application

Being able to look at the past and better understand a situation, the strategies used, and the impact of decisions can help a leader learn what might work best in future situations. It is through learning from failures and successes of the past that leaders can better lead in future leadership situations.

Jocelyn is a new peer advisor responsible for meeting one-on-one every other week with ten first-year students to help them transition to college. She has thought a lot about her experience as a first-year student, and although her position requires her to connect only every other week with her students, Jocelyn remembered what an impact it had on her to connect with her peer advisor weekly to get campus updates and have someone to talk to about the transition. Because of this impact, Jocelyn decides to offer weekly meetings for her students.

Reflection and Application Competencies

Understands the value of reflecting on experiences to apply learning in the future (Knowledge):

Understanding how valuable reflection is in learning from experiences and then using this learning to shape future actions.

Values reflecting on experiences to apply learning in the future (Value):

Believing that there is something to be learned from each experience that can be used to help shape one's future actions and that there is great value in learning from one's mistakes and one's successes and then acting upon that learning in the future.

Motivated to reflect on experiences to apply learning in the future (Ability):

Being motivated to engage in reflection, including thinking about the positive and negative aspects of an experience, to find out what one can do to best shape future actions.

Reflects on experiences to apply learning in the future (Behavior):

Reflecting on experiences, considering the learning gained through reflection, and acting in accordance with this learning.

Related Competency Areas

- Evaluation
- Decision Making

CAS Domain Translation

- Cognitive Complexity

Leadership Model Translation

- Relational Leadership Model: Process Oriented
- Social Change Model of Leadership: Consciousness of Self
- Five Practices of Exemplary Leadership: Challenge the Process

Reflection and Application Curricular Ideas

Dimension(s)	Curriculum	Other Competency Areas Developed
Knowledge	Have students discuss the importance of reflection; why would a leader want to reflect?	
Knowledge	Help students develop a reflection rubric to use as a tool that includes questions they can ask themselves to help them thoughtfully reflect on an experience.	
Value	Have students discuss a time that reflecting on an experience and then applying the learning was valuable to the outcome and/or process.	
Ability	Have students discuss a time that they learned a lesson and how that lesson affected their future behavior.	
Behavior	Have students engage in journaling with prompt questions that get them to think about positives, negatives, and what they may do differently after a significant personal experience.	Evaluation
Behavior	Have students debrief a program or event they put on to discuss what went well, what did not, and what should be changed. If possible, give them an opportunity to apply their findings to the next program or event they conduct and debrief how well they applied those changes.	Evaluation Decision Making

Systems Thinking

Leadership is about networks: individual, organizational, and community. A decision by one can have an impact far beyond the immediate scope of the decision maker. Therefore, leaders must be able to understand how networks work and be able to navigate through both the ripple effects of others' decisions as well as engage in their own decision making that considers the impact on a larger network or system.

The student government on campus has just decided to try to get every first-year student into an organization upon arriving to campus. The student government, through marketing and other initiatives, is aiming for 85 percent of first-year students to join an organization in the first year of the plan's implementation. This is 40 percent higher than the number of first-year students who joined the previous year. It isn't until Reed, a senior, points out that if all the spaces for every organization are filled by first-year

(Continued)

students, three major impacts will arise. First, there will not be any room for students who are not first-year students to join. Second, what will happen next year and the two years following when there is little room in these organizations for new students because this incoming class will comprise the majority of membership? Finally, what happens in four years when these students graduate, possibly resulting in the collapse of some organizations that would graduate the majority of their membership? After sharing this with student government, the group realizes the downsides of their plan and decides to take a step back in terms of their ambitious recruitment of first-year students into organizations.

Systems Thinking Competencies
Understands that individual parts are connected within a larger system (Knowledge):

Understanding that larger systems are made up of individual parts and there is a relationship (cause and effect) between these individual parts; altering one may have an effect on another part and the system as a whole.

Values the understanding that individual parts are connected within a larger system (Value):

Believing that to solve complex problems one must recognize the interrelationship of parts rather than looking at each discrete part within a larger system; this type of thinking allows one to derive a solution that addresses the underlying problem and is less likely to have a negative impact on other parts of the system.

Motivated to make connections of individual parts within a larger system (Ability):

Being motivated to understand how individual parts of a system are connected to each other and to use that understanding to anticipate the impact that altering one part has on other parts and the system as a whole.

Makes connections of individual parts within a larger system (Behavior):

Making connections between individual parts in a system to anticipate how the relationships between these parts affect each part and the system as a whole.

Related Competency Areas

- Analysis
- Problem Solving

- Decision Making
- Creating Change

CAS Domain Translation

- Cognitive Complexity

Leadership Model Translation

- Relational Leadership Model: Process-Oriented
- Social Change Model of Leadership: Citizenship
- Emotionally Intelligent Leadership: Environmental Awareness; Consciousness of Context

Systems Thinking Curricular Ideas

Dimension(s)	Curriculum	Other Competency Areas Developed
Knowledge	Have students look for news stories that reflect interrelated systems and identify all the relationships between components discussed in each story.	
Value	Have students reflect on the actions they took through the course of one day and anticipate what impact their individual actions may have had on a system-wide basis. Have them share with others whether they would act differently after analyzing their experiences through a systems lens.	Reflection and Application Analysis
Ability	Have students engage in a case study in which they come up with a solution to a problem. Then, have them uncover all the unintended consequences on other parts of the system that may be caused by implementing their proposed solution. Have them make alterations to their proposed solution based on the unintended consequences they uncovered with their original solution.	Problem Solving
Behavior	Have students break down a complex problem into smaller components and then describe the causal relationships between each component.	Analysis

Analysis

Leaders are confronted every day with decisions that may have a large impact financially, organizationally, politically, socially, and/or interpersonally. With this responsibility comes the great need to understand a situation in its entirety, all the individual pieces as well as the whole, to make meaning of the situation and make the best decision possible.

As a peer facilitator of the workshop on creating a vision at the annual leadership retreat, Kim was confused as to why the students were not understanding how to create a vision statement after an hour of talking about it. After the retreat, Kim decides to look at the curriculum of the workshop to see whether the method of explaining vision statements was unclear. She determines that the information was spelled out pretty clearly and she presented it straight out of the curriculum. How could they not have gotten it? She then decides to ask the retreat director to share what was covered in the other workshops at the retreat. After looking through the curriculum for these workshops, she finds out that the workshop presenter right before her talked about vision as well but used a different model. No wonder the students were confused; they had just received prior information that wasn't in alignment with her information. Kim's ability to look at the entirety, as well as the individual components of the situation, allowed her to uncover why the students were struggling in understanding the content and the importance of finding out in advance the material that will be covered at the retreat so that her information aligns with the rest of the information presented.

Analysis Competencies

Understands how to analyze information for more thorough understanding (Knowledge):

Understanding how to divide information into smaller components for critical examination in an effort to identify causes, factors, features, and impacts of the information as a whole.

Values analyzing information for more thorough understanding (Value):

Believing that dividing information into smaller components for critical examination can be helpful in understanding both the individual pieces as well as the information as a whole and may be able to shed light on elements of the information that might not have been readily seen if one had not examined each component separately.

Has skills to analyze information for more thorough understanding (Ability):

Being able to divide information into smaller components for critical examination in an effort to identify causes, factors, features, and impacts of the information as a whole.

Analyzes information for more thorough understanding (Behavior): Dividing and examining information in detail to have a more comprehensive understanding of the information as a whole.

Related Competency Areas

- Systems Thinking
- Evaluation
- Decision Making

CAS Domain Translation

- Cognitive Complexity

Leadership Model Translation

- Relational Leadership Model: Purposeful; Process-Oriented
- Emotionally Intelligent Leadership: Consciousness of Context

Analysis Curricular Ideas

Dimension(s)	Curriculum	Other Competency Areas Developed
Knowledge	Present elements of critical analysis and share with students guiding questions that might help them understand how to analyze information.	Evaluation
Value	Have students reflect on a time that engaging in analysis was personally valuable. How did analyzing assist them?	
Ability	Give each student a piece of information from a case study that is part of a larger picture. Have them work as a group to put the information together to make meaning of the larger picture and discuss actions they would take regarding the case study given all the information they know.	Decision Making
Behavior	Have students examine a news story from a variety of lenses, such as human relations, environmental, and economic.	
Behavior	Have students analyze a problem or issue in an organization or group they are a part of and then suggest a solution to the issue.	Problem Solving

Synthesis

As the creation of information continues to grow, the demand for effectively managing that information is a necessary function of leadership.

Leaders must be able to look at a variety of information, some seemingly unrelated, and connect that information to make sense of the bigger picture so that effective and sustainable decisions can be made.

Rashid is a resident assistant (RA) who is planning a program for his residence hall on the topic of solar energy. He is very excited about this but doesn't know the best way to go about putting on the program and getting a good turnout. He knows that four RAs in other residence halls have already put on programs about solar energy. He asks each of them for their evaluations and tries to look for themes across the information that might help him put on a successful program. First, he notices that students who attended a program that had an interactive component noted that they learned a lot about solar energy, whereas the one program that wasn't interactive did not have nearly as high of a rating for learning about solar energy. Two of the programs showed clips from a video that students mostly indicated not enjoying or learning a lot from. Finally, Rashid looks at the suggestions and notices that the majority of participants suggested going to see an actual solar panel setup. With this information, Rashid determines that he would like to do an interactive program that involves taking students to see solar energy at work.

Synthesis Competencies
Understands how to synthesize multiple pieces of information (Knowledge):
Understanding how to integrate separate elements into one whole in that the whole is a single unit versus a collection of individual pieces; understanding how to identify a central theme that emerges from the integration of all the information.

Values synthesizing multiple pieces of information (Value):
Believing that integrating multiple pieces of information into one unit can help determine a central theme, giving one a perspective that would not otherwise emerge if each piece of information were examined discretely.

Has skills to synthesize multiple pieces of information (Ability):
Being able to identify a central theme by integrating separate elements into one unified whole.

Synthesizes multiple pieces of information (Behavior):
Identifying a central theme by integrating separate elements into one unified whole.

Related Competency Areas

- Systems Thinking
- Analysis
- Evaluation

CAS Domain Translation

- Cognitive Complexity

Leadership Model Translation

- Relational Leadership Model: Purposeful; Process-Oriented

Synthesis Curricular Ideas

Dimension(s)	Curriculum	Other Competency Areas Developed
Knowledge	Print out a transcript from a radio interview to see if any themes emerge related to the topic. Themes are subtopics or particular ideas that arise more than once. Assign each theme a color and then highlight the text in the transcript for each theme. Then have students review the colored transcript and try to figure out what themes each color might represent.	
Value	Have students come up with a list of reasons why being able to synthesize is important for a leader.	
Ability	Give students two interview transcripts about the same topic from an online news site. Have them practice highlighting similar concepts between the two interviews using a color-coding system. Then, have them compare their color coding with each other to see if they were able to find all the similar concepts.	Analysis
Behavior	Give students three concepts or objects that are unlike each other and ask them to identify what they all have in common.	
Behavior	Have students read three different articles about a topic and write a one-paragraph summary that captures the essence of all three articles.	Analysis Writing
Behavior	Have students conduct an open-ended survey and identify the most common themes among the responses.	Research

Evaluation

Leaders make difficult decisions every day. In order to make the best decision possible, leaders must be able to sift through a vast array of information with a critical eye, determining the use and importance of every piece of information received. Leaders must be able to look at all of this information and determine which information has the most impact on their situation and which information is just interesting. Navigating through this vast array of information and determining what is useful, to what extent, and how it is useful can help inform the leaders in making effective decisions.

The Earth Day Club just finished its annual Save the Earth Day, an event held at a nearby park with programs designed to help students to better understand the environment and to engage in recycling practices. In the meeting following this event, the group decides to do their own evaluation of the event before looking at the evaluations the participants filled out. They brainstorm what they thought went well, what they thought did not go well, and based on this information, any changes they would like to see for next year's event. Although the list for what did not go well was long, the group determines that some of their ideas, like limited parking at the park, would not affect the event location in the future because the positive aspects of that location far outweighed the drawback of limited parking. Then, they look at the participants' evaluations and determine what information supported their evaluations, what feedback is valuable for next year's planning, and what feedback is not useful. The group is able to leave their meeting with a plan for how they intend to proceed in the future given their reflection on this year's event, knowing that some information is much more valuable than other information.

Evaluation Competencies
Understands how to evaluate information effectively (Knowledge):
Understanding how to use one's judgment to estimate the significance of particular information, thus determining its value.

Values evaluating information effectively (Value):
Believing that information has degrees of value depending on the context and that it is important to use one's judgment to determine to what extent and how the information may be valuable in a particular context.

Has skills to evaluate information effectively (Ability):
Being able to use one's judgment to estimate the significance of particular information, thus determining its value.

Evaluates information effectively (Behavior):

Using one's judgment to estimate the significance of particular information in a specific context, thus determining its value.

Related Competency Areas

- Analysis
- Problem Solving
- Decision Making

CAS Domain Translation

- Cognitive Complexity

Leadership Model Translation

- Relational Leadership Model: Purposeful; Process-Oriented

Evaluation Curricular Ideas

Dimension(s)	Curriculum	Other Competency Areas Developed
Knowledge	Present elements of critical evaluation and share with students guiding questions that might help them understand how to effectively evaluate information.	
Value	Have students share experiences in which their engagement in evaluation helped create future improvements.	Reflection and Application
Ability	Give students a case study and have them identify the three most important aspects related to the case that one must consider before formulating a solution. Have them compare with other groups to see if they came up with the same information.	Analysis
Ability	Give students a case study with three different solutions. Have them determine which is the best solution given the context of the case study. Have each case study group share what they selected and why.	Analysis
Behavior	Give students responses to open-ended questions from a survey and ask them to identify the three most important pieces of information found within the surveys.	Analysis

Idea Generation

Leadership issues are complex; they can involve a variety of people, perspectives, and circumstances. This complexity often does not call for a one-size-fits-all approach. Therefore, it is vital that leaders are able to generate new ideas that effectively address issues in an ever-changing landscape.

Megan is a peer educator who facilitates workshops on various leadership topics. The workshop curriculum is already written and is designed with an undergraduate population as the target audience. However, she is planning on presenting a time management workshop to a visiting group of high school students and is concerned that the activities that were designed for college students will not be appropriate or relevant for a high school demographic. So, Megan thinks about the high school context and comes up with ideas for activities that fit better with what high school students need to know about time management.

Idea Generation Competencies

Understands the value of generating new ideas (Knowledge):

Understanding that leadership issues are contextual and set in an ever-changing landscape, so one must think beyond convention to generate ideas that best address each issue at hand; understanding that one size does not necessarily fit all.

Values generating new ideas (Value):

Believing that leadership issues are contextual and set in an ever-changing landscape, so one must think beyond convention to generate ideas that best address each issue at hand; believing that one size does not necessarily fit all.

Motivated to generate new ideas (Ability):

Being motivated to generate new ideas by expanding one's thinking beyond convention in order to best address an issue; going beyond one-size-fits-all.

Generates new ideas (Behavior):

Generating new ideas by expanding one's thinking beyond convention.

Related Competency Areas

- Research
- Reflection and Application
- Analysis

- Evaluation
- Problem Solving
- Decision Making

CAS Domain Translation

- Knowledge Acquisition, Integration, Construction, and Application

Leadership Model Translation

- Relational Leadership Model: Purposeful; Process-Oriented
- Five Practices of Exemplary Leadership: Challenge the Process
- Emotionally Intelligent Leadership: Change Agent

Idea Generation Curricular Ideas

Dimension(s)	Curriculum	Other Competency Areas Developed
Knowledge Value	Ask students to reflect on the benefits of generating new ideas. Have them think about an idea they developed and the benefits of that idea.	
Ability	Have students discuss what motivates them to come up with new ideas.	
Behavior	Give students the opportunity to create their own process, event, or administrative component.	
Behavior	Give students a problem and have them come up with an innovative solution to the problem that cannot be a solution they have heard about before.	Problem Solving
Behavior	Have students develop a model, hypothesis, theory, or framework and back it up with research.	Research
Behavior	Have students refine an existing concept, program, or other element with a new idea.	

Problem Solving

Although everyone is confronted with problems, because leaders are connected to a larger system, problem solving can often have higher stakes for a group or organization. So, the ability to effectively solve problems is paramount for leaders. Effective problem solving has the opportunity to prevent damage, achieve a successful and productive outcome, refrain from negatively affecting others and in some cases positively affect others, and prevent a problem from reoccurring.

Wendy is part of the Homecoming Committee, and after months of detailed planning, it is one day away from the homecoming festivities. That day, the committee receives 1,000 homecoming shirts to sell the next day. The committee had borrowed $5,000 from student government to pre-pay for the shirts, knowing that they would be able to sell them and more than make up for the money they borrowed. Upon closer inspection of the shirt, Wendy, who was not on the shirt subcommittee, notices a subtle racial slur on the shirt as it relates to the other team's mascot. She finds out that the printing of the shirt was authorized by the chair of the subcommittee who had made some last-minute changes to the design on his own. She and others on the Homecoming Committee do not feel comfortable about selling the shirts. She pulls the entire committee together to brainstorm how to handle this problem. Should they not sell the shirts and fundraise all year to pay back Student Government, donate the shirts, cut them up, burn them in a bonfire, sell them anyway, or try to print new shirts? The committee realizes that this would be the first homecoming without T-shirts, so they need to find a way to sell shirts. After looking at all the pros and cons of each possibility, the committee determines that they are going to reprint color over the slur on the T-shirts, and sell the shirts for $1 more to make up for the amount it would cost to have the T-shirt company send the shirts through another round of printing. The committee decides to make the best out of this situation by hosting a contest. When students purchase their shirts, they can write in any nonoffensive, socially just words on the block of color on their shirts to personalize them. Then, the student who comes up with the most creative words wins a prize.

Problem Solving Competencies
Understands how to solve problems effectively (Knowledge):
Understanding how to identify and examine a problem, develop and assess possible solutions, and select the most appropriate solution to the problem.

Values solving problems effectively (Value):
Believing that the best solution to a problem is derived from careful identification and examination of a problem and its possible solutions.

Has skills to solve problems effectively (Ability):
Being able to identify and examine a problem, develop and assess possible solutions, and select the most appropriate solution to the problem.

Solves problems effectively (Behavior):

Identifying and examining a problem, developing and assessing possible solutions, and selecting the most appropriate solution to the problem.

Related Competency Areas

- Analysis
- Evaluation
- Decision Making

CAS Domain Translation

- Cognitive Complexity

Leadership Model Translation

- Relational Leadership Model: Purposeful; Process-Oriented
- Social Change Model of Leadership: Controversy with Civility
- Five Practices of Exemplary Leadership: Challenge the Process
- Emotionally Intelligent Leadership: Change Agent

Problem-Solving Curricular Ideas

Dimension(s)	Curriculum	Other Competency Areas Developed
Knowledge	Go over different problem types and the problem-solving process.	
Value	Have students reflect on a time that they effectively solved a problem. What can they learn from that situation that they could apply in a similar situation? Then, have the students reflect on a time that they did not effectively solve a problem. What could they have done differently? How important was effective problem solving in these situations?	Reflection and Application Evaluation
Ability	Give students a list of "problems" (or have them generate their own) and have them identify the problem type, factors affecting the problem, and stakeholders to the problem.	Analysis

(Continued)

Problem-Solving Curricular Ideas (Continued)

Dimension(s)	Curriculum	Other Competency Areas Developed
Ability	Have students develop three possible solutions to a problem that they have defined and examined, keeping in mind the context, timing, cost, effects on individuals or groups, and unintended consequences of each solution.	Analysis Idea Generation
Ability	Have students analyze a case study in which a problem and solution are both presented. They should critique the solution in terms of the context, timing, cost, effects on individuals or groups, and unintended consequences. Using their critique, have them consider other solutions that minimize the concerns that emerged from the critique.	Analysis Evaluation Idea Generation
Behavior	Invite students to be a part of real-life problem-solving processes such as setting departmental budgets, developing strategic plans, creating changes to programs or processes, and so on.	

Decision Making

Leaders are continually engaged in leadership situations that require decisions to be made. Each decision to be made is situated in a context that includes factors affecting a specific decision, such as people involved or affected, time, and resources. Understanding this context can help a leader make the most effective, productive, and sustainable decision appropriate for that exact situation.

Jack was a founding member of the Recycling Club and has been a member for three years—longer than anyone else in the club. He is currently the vice president in charge of publicity and communication with the Campus Recycling Department. Jack is not very efficient, has not kept up with his duties, and has created numerous problems that the group has not addressed because of their personal liking for him. Several members of the club, though, have had enough and want Jack removed from his vice president position. Susie, the president, has talked to Jack on a number of occasions about his performance, but nothing has changed. The executive board decides to meet and discuss Jack's role, considering that if they ask him to resign his position, he will most likely not participate in the Recycling Club any longer; also, his involvement in the Recycling Club as vice president is part of an internship he is doing for credits in order to graduate in May. Based on this information, the executive board decides to remove Jack from his role as vice president but give him special duties that capture his historical knowledge of the organization, such as creating the club's website and operations manual so he can leave his legacy on the organization as well as fulfill his internship duties.

Decision Making Competencies
Understands the value of making decisions appropriate to each situation (Knowledge):
Understanding that each situation has a context and that it is important to make each decision appropriate to the context it is situated in.

Values making decisions appropriate to each situation (Value):
Believing that it is important to make each decision appropriate to the context it is situated in.

Motivated to make decisions appropriate to each situation (Ability):
Being motivated to make decisions appropriate to the context it is situated in.

Makes decisions appropriate to each situation (Behavior):
Making each decision appropriate to the context it is situated in.

Related Competency Areas
- Analysis
- Evaluation
- Problem Solving

CAS Domain Translation
- Cognitive Complexity

Leadership Model Translation
- Relational Leadership Model: Purposeful; Process-Oriented
- Social Change Model of Leadership: Controversy with Civility

Decision-Making Curricular Ideas

Dimension(s)	Curriculum	Other Competency Areas Developed
Knowledge	Share with students techniques for effective decision making. Have students contribute by sharing techniques that have worked for them.	
Value	Have students reflect on a bad decision (not just a decision resulting in a negative outcome) and a good decision (not just a decision resulting in a positive outcome) and have them analyze what made the decision bad or good.	Analysis
Ability	Give students a case study and have them brainstorm all the contextual factors influencing the case.	Analysis
Ability	Give students a case study and three different possibilities of decisions that could have been made to address the issue in the case study. Have them weigh the pros and cons of these potential decisions in the context of the case study.	Analysis Evaluation
Behavior	Have students role-play a scenario in which they must "make a decision." Students should use their roles and the interactions among the group during the scenario to create context for this decision. After they are done role-playing, have them assess the appropriateness of the decision enacted.	Evaluation

Chapter 2

Self-Awareness and Development

Self-Understanding

Self-awareness is vital to effective leadership. Not understanding how one might respond to change or working from one's weaknesses while thinking they are strengths can have devastating impacts on others. However, when a leader understands his or her feelings, beliefs, actions, skills, and personality, he or she can emphasize strengths and mitigate weaknesses in his or her leadership style and lead with more authenticity and in a more productive manner.

Kelly, the new student manager of the copy center on campus, just got back from a training session on dealing with stress. At this seminar, Kelly discovered that one of the ways that she handles stress is to ask a lot of questions—sometimes over and over again and usually questions she knows the answer to. She never realized that she did this before the training but was able to confirm this behavior by asking others afterward if they had seen her engage in this behavior during stressful situations. In the training, Kelly learned that if she is stressed, one way she can de-stress is by taking time away from a situation. Knowing that her position is in a high-stress environment, she knows that her typical behavior may create a situation in which her employees doubt her knowledge to do the job and then may not seek her out for support or guidance. Kelly now knows that when she is feeling stressed, she will refrain from asking everyone an excessive number of questions and instead will take a step outside until she de-stresses.

Self-Understanding Competencies
Understands oneself (Knowledge):
Being aware of one's own personality, beliefs, capacities, and interests.

Values understanding oneself (Value):
Believing that it is important to be aware of one's own personality, beliefs, capacities, and interests in an effort to engage in more authentic and productive behavior.

Motivated to enhance the understanding of oneself (Ability):
Being motivated to enhance one's understanding of one's personality, beliefs, capacities, and interests so as to develop a greater depth of understanding of oneself in order to engage in more authentic and productive behavior.

Enhances the understanding of oneself (Behavior):
Enhancing one's understanding of one's personality, beliefs, capacities, and interests.

Related Competency Areas
- Personal Values
- Personal Contributions
- Self-Development
- Confidence

CAS Domain Translation
- Intrapersonal Development

Leadership Model Translation
- Relational Leadership Model: Inclusive
- Social Change Model of Leadership: Consciousness of Self
- Five Practices of Exemplary Leadership: Model the Way
- Emotionally Intelligent Leadership: Honest Self-Understanding

Self-Understanding Curricular Ideas

Dimension(s)	Curriculum	Other Competency Areas Developed
Knowledge	Ask students to reflect on an experience and interpret their behavior in terms of their values, goals, and styles. What shaped how they behaved?	Personal Values
Knowledge	Ask students to reflect on a time they were a member of a successful team. Ask them to share with others how they contributed to the success of that team.	Personal Contributions
Knowledge	Have students take assessments to learn about their own styles (communication, conflict, personality, leadership, and so on).	
Value	Have students brainstorm reasons why understanding oneself can be valuable as a leader.	
Value	Have students reflect on a time when not knowing something about their own personalities, beliefs, capacities, or interests hindered their ability as a leader and a time when knowing something about their own personality, beliefs, capacities, or interests helped them to be a better leader.	Reflection and Application
Ability	Have students share what motivates them in learning more about themselves.	
Behavior	Have students complete a forced rank or forced continuum exercise that highlights a variety of beliefs and values. Ask them to reflect on why they answered the way they did.	Evaluation
Behavior	Have students discuss a controversial issue. Process by asking what aspects of their values and opinions shaped their role during the discussion as well as what feelings emerged for them during the discussion.	Personal Values

Personal Values

Values are a guiding force for individual behavior. Being aware of one's own values can help a leader prioritize organizational initiatives and make decisions aligned with those values. And, leaders who demonstrate their values through leadership can inspire others to work with them.

David is running for NPHC (National Pan-Hellenic Council) president and decides that he wants to be transparent with the members of NPHC so they are clear from the beginning what his values are. He does not want to waver to appease everyone. So, David lays out his top three values—collaboration, honesty, and loyalty—and then ties them to how he would approach the important issues facing NPHC. He knows that there has been on-and-off collaboration between fraternities and sororities in NPHC and members of other Greek governing organizations on campus. He truly believes that the strength of the fraternity and sorority system comes from working together on joint initiatives. He decides that his campaign message will be sharing his commitment to collaboration among all fraternities and sororities and designs all of his speeches and campaign material around collaboration. He even works to collaborate with executive officers in each of the fraternities and sororities to come up with ideas for what they could do together if he is elected. Many individuals in NPHC, even those who have never met him, jump on board because they believe this is the direction that NPHC needs to go, and they believe that David's demonstration of collaboration during the campaign will carry over to his motivation to collaborate once elected. David knows he took a risk by putting his values out there, but he believes that his presidency will be authentic only if he leads with his values.

Personal Values Competencies

Understands the value of acting in alignment with one's own values (Knowledge):

Understanding that acting in alignment with one's own values can contribute to one's authenticity as well as inspire others.

Values acting in alignment with one's own values (Value):

Believing that acting in alignment with one's own values can contribute to one's authenticity as well as inspire others.

Motivated to act in alignment with one's own values (Ability):

Being motivated to act in alignment with one's own values can contribute to one's authenticity and ability to inspire others.

Acts in alignment with one's own values (Behavior):

Acting in alignment with one's own values.

Related Competency Areas

- Decision Making
- Self-Understanding
- Ethics

CAS Domain Translation

- Intrapersonal Development

Leadership Model Translation

- Relational Leadership Model: Ethical

- Social Change Model of Leadership: Congruence; Commitment

- Five Practices of Exemplary Leadership: Model the Way

- Emotionally Intelligent Leadership: Honest Self-Understanding; Consciousness of Self

Personal Values Curricular Ideas

Dimension(s)	Curriculum	Other Competency Areas Developed
Knowledge	Have students reflect on a decision they made in the past and uncover how their values may have affected the decision.	Reflection and Application
Knowledge Value	Have students define the five most important values in their lives and share with someone as to why those are their most important values. How have those values affected their actions?	Evaluation Self-Understanding
Value	Have students share how understanding their values has helped them be better leaders.	
Value	Have students share a time they made a decision that went against their values, and have them discuss the result of that decision and how the decision-making process made them feel.	
Ability	Give each student an individual case study. Have them decide how they would approach the situation in the case study and then reflect on how their values would have played a role in the decisions they would make regarding the case.	Analysis Decision Making
Behavior	Ask students to spend the day trying to live out their top five values. Then, have them report back about the experience.	

Personal Contributions

Everyone has assets, those aspects of themselves that are helpful and contributory, including ideas, strengths, knowledge, and abilities. Leaders who know what their assets are can tap into them to lead more effectively.

A leader who contributes the strength of compassion when someone in the group falls on hard times can positively affect others, or a leader who contributes the ability of website design when others in the organization lack that ability can contribute positively to a needed task. Leaders give of themselves to make their organizations better.

Fabiola is an amazing visionary. She has been told by others that if they need to brainstorm ideas, they go to her first. She has a way of being able not only to share her ideas but ask the right questions of others to get them to share their ideas and build momentum off others' ideas. Fabiola has just joined a new organization, Business Students for Change. The organization is brand new and just forming its mission, structure, and identity. For weeks now, Fabiola has been sitting in the meetings watching the new president struggle to get the group to come up with ideas for a mission statement. It appears that the group has ideas, but the process is not going very smoothly, resulting in few people sharing. Fabiola asks the president after one of the meetings if she could facilitate the discussion about the mission statement at the next meeting. The president, although surprised by the question, is not reluctant at all to give someone else a chance to move the group forward. During the next meeting, Fabiola uses her strength of facilitating the visioning process to get the group discussing and finalizing a mission statement that reflects the ideas of the entire group.

Personal Contributions Competencies
Understands the value of offering one's own contributions (Knowledge):

Understanding that the needs of each group and each task differ and call for unique individual assets to best address these needs; thus, contributing one's own ideas, strengths, knowledge, and/or abilities to meet a specific need can be valuable in enhancing the productivity and effectiveness of the group.

Values offering one's own contributions (Value):

Believing that the needs of each group and each task differ and call for unique individual assets to best address these needs; thus, contributing one's own ideas, strengths, knowledge, and/or abilities to meet a specific need can be valuable in enhancing the productivity and effectiveness of the group.

Motivated to offer one's own contributions (Ability):

Being motivated to contribute one's own ideas, strengths, knowledge, and/or abilities to meet a specific group need.

Offers one's own contributions (Behavior):

Contributing one's own ideas, strengths, knowledge, and/or abilities to meet a specific group need.

Related Competency Areas

- Self-Understanding
- Scope of Competence
- Helping Others
- Confidence

CAS Domain Translation

- Intrapersonal Development

Leadership Model Translation

- Relational Leadership Model: Empowering
- Social Change Model of Leadership: Consciousness of Self
- Five Practices of Exemplary Leadership: Model the Way; Enable Others to Act
- Emotionally Intelligent Leadership: Honest Self-Understanding

Personal Contributions Curricular Ideas

Dimension(s)	Curriculum	Other Competency Areas Developed
Knowledge	Have students create an asset map of their strengths, knowledge, and abilities and reflect on how contributing these assets could benefit a current task or relationship.	Self-Development
Value	Have students share a time that they contributed an idea, strength, knowledge, or ability to benefit an individual, group, or community. How did it make them feel about themselves to offer that idea, strength, or ability? What was the impact on others?	
Ability	Have students reflect on a time that they could have contributed an idea, strength, or ability to an individual, group, or community but chose not to. Ask them to think about what held them back from doing so and what could have helped motivate them to contribute.	

(Continued)

Personal Contributions Curricular Ideas (Continued)

Dimension(s)	Curriculum	Other Competency Areas Developed
Ability	Ask students to reflect on a current group they are involved with. Have them assess the needs of the group and how their personal assets (ideas, strengths, knowledge, and abilities) could contribute to the group. Then, have them make a plan to start contributing those assets.	Evaluation Plan
Behavior	Give students a case study in which there is an issue with a multitude of factors. Have them brainstorm ideas to address the issue. After, have them reflect on how they contributed to the discussion, what they chose to contribute and what they did not, and what their process was for contributing.	Analysis

Scope of Competence

Engaging in a task outside one's capabilities can have harmful effects on others and organizations. Just as it is important to know one's own strengths, skills, and talents that one may bring to a situation, it is just as vital for a leader to know what he or she does not bring to the situation. By recognizing one's own limitations, the leader can engage in those tasks that he or she is capable of and refer those outside of his or her scope of competence to others more competent at the task at hand.

Bobby is the marketing chair for the Hall Council, in charge of marketing all the residence hall events to the students who live in the hall. He is a marketing major and is excited about this opportunity to come up with great marketing ideas. Upon presenting his ideas to the rest of Hall Council, the council decides to add more marketing strategies to his list, one of which is monitoring the hall discussion boards online. Bobby has never done this type of task before, and he is much more skilled in and interested in the development of the monthly hall newsletter. Bobby doesn't say anything to anyone about this and believes he can get on board and try to monitor the discussion board himself without any training. When he logs in for the first time, he sees that someone had posted a scathing comment about one of the staff members that he knows needs to be removed right away. Because he knows his skill limitations in monitoring the discussion board, he refers the issue to the Hall Council president, who knows how to quickly resolve the situation. Bobby learns that he needs to speak up sooner so he can either defer the task to someone else or be trained to do it effectively to avoid situations like this in the future.

Scope of Competence Competencies

Understands the value of acting within the scope of one's own competencies when outside of a learning environment (Knowledge):

Understanding that we all have limitations and that some tasks are best suited for those who have a more appropriate level of competence than one's own for that task; it is important to be aware of the extent of one's competencies in an effort to not take on more than one is capable of.

Values acting within the scope of one's own competencies when outside of a learning environment (Value):

Believing that we all have limitations and that some tasks are best suited for those who have a more appropriate level of competence for that task; it is important to be aware of the extent of one's competencies in an effort to not take on more than one is capable of.

Motivated to act within the scope of one's own competencies when outside of a learning environment (Ability):

Being motivated to not engage in tasks outside of one's competency level and to refer a task to someone else when one does not have the adequate competency level to engage effectively in that task, so as to not take on more than one is capable of and to have the task be completed most effectively.

Acts within the scope of one's own competencies when outside of a learning environment (Behavior):

Not engaging in tasks outside of one's competency level and referring these tasks to those who have the competency level necessary to effectively complete the task.

Related Competency Areas

- Evaluation
- Self-Understanding
- Personal Contributions
- Self-Development

CAS Domain Translation

- Intrapersonal Development

Leadership Model Translation

- Relational Leadership Model: Inclusive; Empowering

- Social Change Model of Leadership: Consciousness of Self; Commitment
- Five Practices of Exemplary Leadership: Model the Way; Enable Others to Act
- Emotionally Intelligent Leadership: Honest Self-Understanding; Consciousness of Self

Scope of Competence Curricular Ideas

Dimension(s)	Curriculum	Other Competency Areas Developed
Knowledge	Have students self-assess their competencies, focusing on skills necessary for an important role they are in. Have them assess to what extent they have these skills.	Evaluation Self-Understanding
Value	Have students reflect on a time that they took on a task that called for a particular competency that they did not possess. Ask them to share the impact of that situation and to brainstorm additional challenges that could have arisen in the situation.	Self-Understanding
Value	Have students share a time when someone else took on a task that they didn't have the competency level for and the impact that this had on the situation.	
Ability	Have students share a time they were asked to engage in a task that they did not have the competency level for. If they engaged in the task, what motivated them to do so? If they did not, what motivated them to not engage in it?	
Behavior	Have students document the times throughout one week that they refer a task to another person because either they do not have the necessary competency level for it or another person has a greater competency level for it. Have the students report back about the experience.	

Receiving Feedback

For a leader to continue to develop as well as enhance his or her effectiveness with others, being self-aware is essential. Sometimes, however, a leader cannot simply self-assess his or her own competencies or behavior because there are elements that are not visible to the leader in the same way as they are to others. So, these areas often either go unaddressed or are not addressed in the best manner. Being able to consider feedback from others is crucial for a leader to best develop his or her competencies and increase his or her effectiveness with others.

Andy is a teaching assistant for a leadership class. He presents some material, grades assignments, and works with students one-on-one as needed. This is Andy's first experience in a role like this, and he wants to do the best job possible. Midway through the semester, the instructor hands out a survey to the students to gather feedback about Andy's effectiveness in the teaching assistant role so that Andy can both learn from the experience and make any necessary changes in the class before the end of the semester. After the instructor reads through the survey responses, she summarizes the feedback for Andy and accentuates the areas in which he is doing well and helps him think of strategies to address his potential growth areas.

Receiving Feedback Competencies
Understands the value of considering feedback from others (Knowledge):
Understanding that feedback from others can be important in developing one's own capacity and increasing effectiveness with others.

Values considering feedback from others (Value):
Believing that feedback from others is important to develop one's own capacity and increase effectiveness with others.

Motivated to consider feedback from others (Ability):
Being motivated to consider feedback from others in an effort to develop one's own capacity and increase effectiveness with others.

Considers feedback from others (Behavior):
Considering feedback from others.

Related Competency Areas
- Self-Understanding
- Scope of Competence
- Self-Development
- Excellence

CAS Domain Translation
- Intrapersonal Development

Leadership Model Translation

- Relational Leadership Model: Process-Oriented
- Social Change Model of Leadership: Consciousness of Self; Controversy with Civility
- Five Practices of Exemplary Leadership: Model the Way
- Emotionally Intelligent Leadership: Honest Self-Understanding; Flexibility

Receiving Feedback Curricular Ideas

Dimension(s)	Curriculum	Other Competency Areas Developed
Knowledge	Have students discuss why getting feedback is important.	
Knowledge	Share how to get valuable and useful feedback from others.	
Value	Have students reflect on a time that they were given valuable constructive feedback and how that feedback shaped their future behaviors and self-development.	Self-Understanding
Value	Have students reflect on a time that they were given valuable positive feedback and how that feedback shaped their future behaviors and self-development.	Self-Understanding
Value	Ask the students to think about a time that they received feedback they didn't like but realized that it was accurate. Have them share with others why they didn't like getting the feedback.	Self-Understanding
Ability	Ask students to share what motivates them and/or holds them back from seeking feedback from others. How can they be motivated to seek feedback?	
Behavior	Have students give feedback to each other. Ask them how it felt to receive feedback.	Providing Feedback
Behavior	Have students create a feedback tool (evaluation) for a role they are in. Have them use the tool to gather feedback from others about themselves. Then, process how they intend to integrate the feedback into their lives.	Evaluation Excellence

Self-Development

Whether it is learning new technology or how to become a better public speaker, leaders are always learning. They may do this voluntarily, like seeking out training, or out of necessity based on the leader's role or the group's needs.

Rebecca has just been re-elected the communications coordinator in her sorority. She manages the discussion boards and social media sites. The sorority, however, has been outsourcing its website management to someone for $1,000 a year. Rebecca simply sends text updates to the website manager to post on the web. Sometimes, the posting of the information can be delayed by up to a week, so important updates become "old news." Rebecca found out that the only reason the website was outsourced was that no one in the sorority knows how to build and manage a website. Realizing that not only would it save the sorority $1,000 a year to manage the site internally, they would be able to have more control over the design and certainly the speed at which information was posted. So, Rebecca asked the sorority for $300 to go to a website design class so she could learn how to design and manage the website internally. Not only will the sorority benefit, but now Rebecca will have a new skill set.

Self-Development Competencies
Understands the value of self-development (Knowledge):
Understanding that self-development is important in helping one to achieve one's fullest potential and that the competencies gained or enhanced through self-development can be beneficial to oneself and others.

Values self-development (Value):
Believing that self-development is important in helping one to achieve one's fullest potential and that the competencies gained or enhanced through self-development can be beneficial to oneself and others.

Motivated to engage in self-development (Ability):
Being motivated to engage in self-development opportunities to achieve one's fullest potential and benefit oneself and others.

Engages in self-development (Behavior):
Engaging in self-development opportunities to develop one's competencies.

Related Competency Areas
- Self-Understanding
- Scope of Competence
- Receiving Feedback
- Excellence

CAS Domain Translation

- Intrapersonal Development

Leadership Model Translation

- Relational Leadership Model: Inclusive

- Social Change Model of Leadership: Consciousness of Self

- Emotionally Intelligent Leadership: Achievement

Self-Development Curricular Ideas

Dimension(s)	Curriculum	Other Competency Areas Developed
Knowledge	Have students identify five competencies they would like to develop. Then, have them discuss all the reasons that developing those competencies would be valuable both to themselves and to organizations they are a part of.	Self-Understanding
Value	Have students list the five competencies they have developed since they have gotten to college that they believe are most beneficial in their lives. Have them share with others why developing these competencies has been beneficial.	
Ability	Have students discuss experiences in which they engaged in self-development. Have them share what the experience was and how it helped them develop.	
Ability	Have students create professional development action plans outlining competencies that they would like to develop. Then, have them find opportunities that would develop each of the competencies on their lists.	Plan
Ability	Ask the students to offer each other ideas on how to develop the competencies they want to develop.	Providing Feedback
Behavior	Have students engage in a self-development experience and share what they learned with others.	

Chapter 3

Interpersonal Interaction

Productive Relationships

Leadership requires that a leader has meaningful connections with others; simply interacting with people does not constitute a relationship. A leader who cultivates productive, mutually beneficial relationships with others can create a trusting environment in which people care about each other. This allows for channels of communication to open for the emergence of new ideas and honest dialogue, a personal and professional support structure to develop, and a shared commitment for a vision or task to be created.

Shelly is the chair of the Leadership Conference Planning Committee. Because this is her third year on the committee, Shelly has always felt that the conference planning committee is her second family. Most of the committee members with whom she felt such a connection have moved on, and their positions have been filled by new members whom she doesn't know well. Shelly knows that in order to pull off this conference, committee members must be able to operate like a family: be honest with each other, feel a sense of commitment not just to the task but to each other, and support each other when certain roles are in their peak task times. She knows that these are things you cannot just tell the committee to do; everyone must want to do them. So, Shelly decides to set up an overnight retreat for the committee to really get to know everyone and have them get to know each other. She and the advisor design icebreakers and team builders to help each person connect with every other person. After they return from the retreat, Shelly notices a remarkable difference in the group. They share ideas more often in the meetings, spend more time together outside of the conference planning, help each other with their tasks, and communicate more frequently with each other.

Productive Relationships Competencies
Understands how to develop productive relationships with others (Knowledge):
Understanding strategies to cultivate connections or associations with others that contribute positively to the well-being of those involved.

Values developing productive relationships with others (Value):
Believing that it is important to cultivate connections or associations with others that contribute positively to the well-being of those involved in order to have a mutual support system and opportunity for meaningful exchange.

Has skills to develop productive relationships with others (Ability):
Being able to cultivate connections or associations with others that contribute positively to the well-being of those involved.

Develops productive relationships with others (Behavior):
Cultivating connections or associations with others that contribute positively to the well-being of those involved.

Related Competency Areas
- Appropriate Interaction
- Collaboration

CAS Domain Translation
- Interpersonal Competence

Leadership Model Translation
- Relational Leadership Model: Process-Oriented
- Social Change Model of Leadership: Collaboration
- Five Practices of Exemplary Leadership: Enable Others to Act; Encourage the Heart
- Emotionally Intelligent Leadership: Developing Relationships; Teamwork

Productive Relationships Curricular Ideas

Dimension(s)	Curriculum	Other Competency Areas Developed
Knowledge	Present strategies to the students about how to develop productive relationships. Have them share strategies they have used to develop productive relationships with others.	
Knowledge	Have students reflect on a relationship they would consider productive and identify the attributes of that relationship. In turn, have them reflect on a relationship they would not consider productive and identify the attributes of that relationship. Have them think about the similarities and differences between both relationships.	
Value	Have students brainstorm all the ways that a particular productive relationship they have with another person has been a positive force in their lives. Have them consider why this relationship is valuable to them.	
Ability	Have students analyze a case study of individuals in productive relationships and those not in productive relationships. Have them identify what makes these relationships productive or not. Then, have them consider options to cultivate the unproductive relationships into productive ones.	Analysis
Ability	Have students think of a relationship that they would like to cultivate and have them outline steps they could take that could develop this relationship into a productive one.	Plan
Behavior	Have students implement the steps they outlined to cultivate a current relationship into a productive one. Have them report back about the effectiveness of the strategies they used and whether, and to what extent, the relationship has improved.	
Behavior	Have students plan and initiate an activity to help build productive relationships within one of the groups with which they are involved.	Plan

Appropriate Interaction

Everyone is different, whether because of a situation, a personality, or a set of circumstances. Leaders must understand this context and gauge their interactions to respect the boundaries, needs, and styles of others.

Renee is an orientation leader who works both with prospective students and their families. Two days a week she is with the family program and two days a week she is with the students. Renee knows that both populations are different and that she needs to interact differently with them. The families want more information and reassurance on the academic program, safety, and academic support services like tutoring and library services. The students, however, want more information on campus involvement, athletics, and the residence hall experience. In order to be effective, Renee must be savvy about the way she interacts with both groups of people. So, with the students, she tends to show off her school pride, talk about her own college experiences, and give them insider tips on how to navigate campus. With the families, though, she shares academic statistics and discusses the nuts and bolts of campus: locations of buildings, how students register, financial aid, and campus resources. In addition, her demeanor is different when working with the two different groups. She is much more "student-like" when with the students and much more professional with the families. Her ability to adapt her interactions, both in her style and the content she focuses on, helps make the connections with each group more effective.

Appropriate Interaction Competencies
Understands how to interact with others appropriately (Knowledge):

Understanding strategies to assess a situation and then engaging in interactions, relations, and exchanges based on what is suitable for the context and person or people being interacted with.

Values interacting with others appropriately (Value):

Believing that it is important to assess a situation and engage in interactions, relations, and exchanges based on what is suitable for the context and person or people being interacted with in order to respect boundaries and create an opportunity for the most effective interaction.

Has skills to interact with others appropriately (Ability):

Being able to assess a situation and engage in interactions, relations, and exchanges based on what is suitable for the context and person or people being interacted with.

Interacts with others appropriately (Behavior):

Assessing a situation and engaging in interactions, relations, and exchanges based on what is suitable for the context and person or people being interacted with.

Related Competency Areas

- Evaluation
- Productive Relationships

CAS Domain Translation

- Interpersonal Competence

Leadership Model Translation

- Relational Leadership Model: Process-Oriented
- Social Change Model of Leadership: Controversy with Civility
- Emotionally Intelligent Leadership: Group Savvy

Appropriate Interaction Curricular Ideas

Dimension(s)	Curriculum	Other Competency Areas Developed
Knowledge	Have students discuss ways that they can assess a situation for what might be appropriate or inappropriate behavior.	Evaluation
Knowledge	Have students attend an etiquette seminar discussing topics such as appropriate networking or interview behavior.	
Value	Have students brainstorm the challenges or negative outcomes that can arise from inappropriate interactions with others.	
Value	Have students share experiences in which they did not interact appropriately with someone else given the context of the situation. What was the situation? How did they act? Why did they act that way? What was the impact of their actions?	
Ability	Have students role-play an interaction with someone in an authority position (a potential donor, employer, reporter, instructor, and so on). Give the students feedback on the appropriateness of the interaction.	Receiving Feedback
Ability	Have students respond to case studies that involve appropriate and inappropriate interactions. Have them identify whether the actions were or were not appropriate, and if not, how those interactions could be improved.	Analysis Evaluation
Behavior	Have each student attend a networking reception with another student. Afterward, have them give each other feedback on the appropriateness of their interactions.	Receiving Feedback Providing Feedback

Helping Others

There are times in people's jobs, families, or personal lives in which they could benefit from assistance, whether to make something less difficult or less time consuming. Because leaders care about people, they know how valuable it is to help others and foster an environment in which people help each other.

Leo has just begun his second year working at campus dining and is in charge of stocking the salad bar. Leo spends most of his shifts running from the kitchen to the front of the dining hall; his job may be one of the busiest. During the first week of classes, hundreds of new students come to the dining hall. Many of the other employees in campus dining are just beginning their first week on the job, and with all these students, the dining hall can be a pretty overwhelming and confusing place for new employees. Although Leo is very busy, especially because there are more students at the dining hall this first week than any time during the school year, he still makes time to help his peers be successful in their roles. He checks in with the new employees frequently and answers any question they have. His checking in often leads to explaining processes and sometimes just showing them where things are. This is not Leo's job to do, but he remembers how overwhelming it was when he was a new employee and wants to make sure his peers get the assistance they need.

Helping Others Competencies
Understands the value of helping others beyond one's own responsibilities (Knowledge):
Understanding that it is important to voluntarily give assistance to others when one has no personal stake in the outcome of the assistance so as to make a task or process less difficult or time consuming for others.

Values helping others beyond one's own responsibilities (Value):
Believing that it is important to voluntarily give assistance to others when one has no personal stake in the outcome of the assistance in an effort to make a task or process less difficult or time consuming for others.

Motivated to help others beyond one's own responsibilities (Ability):
Being motivated to voluntarily give assistance to others when one has no personal stake in the outcome of the assistance.

Helps others beyond one's own responsibilities (Behavior):
Voluntarily giving assistance to others when one has no personal stake in the outcome of the assistance.

Related Competency Areas

- Empowerment
- Ethics
- Excellence

CAS Domain Translation

- Interpersonal Competence

Leadership Model Translation

- Relational Leadership Model: Ethical
- Social Change Model of Leadership: Citizenship
- Emotionally Intelligent Leadership: Citizenship; Coaching

Helping Others Curricular Ideas

Dimension(s)	Curriculum	Other Competency Areas Developed
Knowledge	Have students engage in a debate as to whether or not it is possible to altruistically help others.	Verbal Communication Advocating for a Point of View
Value	Have students discuss a time that someone gave them assistance with nothing to gain from the situation. Have them share information on the situation and the impact of the assistance given.	
Value	Have students discuss a time that they gave assistance to someone with nothing to gain. Have them share information on the situation and how their assistance was helpful to the other person.	
Ability	Have students reflect on their motivations to help others, considering factors that support or impede that motivation.	Personal Values
Ability	Have students analyze current events for examples of people helping others when they have nothing personally to gain from that assistance.	Analysis

(Continued)

Helping Others Curricular Ideas (Continued)

Dimension(s)	Curriculum	Other Competency Areas Developed
Ability	Have students observe a crowded area to watch for people helping others, especially those who appear not to know each other. Have them write about or discuss these situations and what they believe the motivation was behind this assistance and the perceived impact of the assistance.	
Ability	Have students create a list of ten things they can do to enhance their motivation to help others.	
Behavior	Have students engage in serving others (community service, acts of kindness, and so on). Have them reflect on the impact this experience had on themselves and others.	Service

Empathy

Empathy plays an important role in leadership. Not only can demonstrating empathy with others build relationships and a sense of trust, it can also help a leader understand another point of view or other set of circumstances to effectively inform the leader's decisions and actions.

Jasper is heading out for a service learning trip to a low-income inner-city area where he and fourteen of his peers are going to do some urban redevelopment, specifically a painting project to cover up graffiti. The group is excited about the trip, especially because some students have never been to this city before. Jasper knows that this is not a vacation and that the work they are doing affects real people. So, for the first two days they are on the trip, Jasper spends a great deal of time talking to the residents of the community and really trying to get a grasp on their perspectives. He hears stories, meets a lot of people, and even gets invited to dinner by one family. He tries to imagine himself in their situations as they describe their concerns. He asks the residents what the students could do on their trip to best help their community. Jasper learns that what the community really wants is to fix up the nearby park so the kids have somewhere safe to play. He can only imagine how challenging it must be to not have anywhere nearby for kids to play safely. Jasper then goes back to the group and explains the concerns of the residents. He asks the group whether they would be willing to spend their last three days fixing up the park. The group agrees, and because of Jasper's ability to understand the concerns of the residents, the park revitalization effort gets under way.

Empathy Competencies

Understands how to demonstrate empathy (Knowledge):

Understanding strategies to demonstrate a deep understanding of others by attempting to experience their thoughts and feelings.

Values demonstrating empathy (Value):

Believing that it is important to demonstrate a deep understanding of others by attempting to experience their thoughts and feelings in an effort to appreciate their perspectives and circumstances as well as show genuine care.

Has skills to demonstrate empathy (Ability):

Being able to demonstrate a deep understanding of others by attempting to experience their thoughts and feelings.

Demonstrates empathy (Behavior):

Demonstrating a deep understanding of others by attempting to experience their thoughts and feelings.

Related Competency Areas

- Other Perspectives
- Decision Making
- Productive Relationships
- Others' Circumstances
- Listening

CAS Domain Translation

- Interpersonal Competence

Leadership Model Translation

- Relational Leadership Model: Empowering; Inclusive
- Five Practices of Exemplary Leadership: Encourage the Heart
- Emotionally Intelligent Leadership: Empathy

Empathy Curricular Ideas

Dimension(s)	Curriculum	Other Competency Areas Developed
Knowledge	Have students brainstorm techniques to authentically imagine themselves in another person's life, including asking questions, deep listening, and thoughtful decision making.	Listening
Value	Have students discuss the role of empathy in decision making.	Decision Making
Value	Have students share what it feels like to have someone empathize with them and the impact this empathy has on the interaction and its outcome.	
Ability	Have students share a time in which they demonstrated empathy. What was their motivation to demonstrate empathy? What techniques did they use to demonstrate empathy?	
Behavior	Have students pair up and engage in a dialogue about a personal issue. During the dialogue, have each try to experience the thoughts and feelings of the other person by asking questions and engaging in deep listening.	Listening

Mentoring

It is vital that leaders share their knowledge, ability, and/or experience with more novice individuals to help them develop their capacities. Doing so is not just good for the individual, but developing the capacities of others could contribute to team productivity, a greater sense of trust, more group legitimacy, and foster thoughtful succession planning.

Joey, the president of the Engineering Club, is passionate about his role and the club in general. He has been a member all four years of college, and although he is excited to graduate from college, he is sad to leave the club. The club executive board decided several years back to hold elections in November so that officers are in their roles from January to January each year. This allows them to work with the outgoing officers for the spring semester to ensure a smooth transition. Upon Caroline's election as club president in November, Joey immediately takes her under his wing: meeting with her to share ideas, projects, and processes as well as introducing her to people in the engineering department whom she would work directly with. Joey even co-facilitates the semester's remaining club meetings so she can practice for when she facilitates them on her own. He wants Caroline to be in the best situation to lead the club effectively after his departure.

Mentoring Competencies
Understands how to mentor others effectively (Knowledge):

Understanding ways to use one's expertise and experience to teach, coach, share resources, and challenge individuals with less experience and/or knowledge to reach their potential.

Values mentoring others effectively (Value):

Believing that it is important to use one's expertise and experience to teach, coach, share resources, and challenge individuals with less experience and/or knowledge to reach their potential.

Has skills to mentor others effectively (Ability):

Being able to use one's expertise and experience to teach, coach, share resources, and challenge individuals with less experience or knowledge to reach their potential.

Mentors others effectively (Behavior):

Using one's expertise and experience to teach, coach, share resources, and challenge individuals with less experience and/or knowledge so that they can reach their potential.

Related Competency Areas

- Productive Relationships
- Motivation
- Empowerment
- Providing Feedback

CAS Domain Translation

- Interpersonal Competence

Leadership Model Translation

- Relational Leadership Model: Empowering
- Five Practices of Exemplary Leadership: Enable Others to Act
- Emotionally Intelligent Leadership: Coaching

Mentoring Curricular Ideas

Dimension(s)	Curriculum	Other Competency Areas Developed
Knowledge	Present strategies students can use to mentor less experienced individuals.	
Knowledge Value	Have students reflect on their mentors and what they have gained from those relationships.	
Value	Have students brainstorm the benefits of mentoring, both generally as well as in a specific context of their choice (career development, within an organization, and so on).	
Ability	Have students think about an area of their lives in which they have experience and/or expertise about something. Have them think about what would be most important to share with individuals who are less experienced or knowledgeable and the best ways to go about sharing that information to help them be successful in this endeavor.	Scope of Competence
Behavior	Have students pair up and each be the expert for a day on something they have knowledge or skills in. Have them help each other develop knowledge or skills related to this expertise (for example, how to bake a pie, how to change a tire, how to make a website). Afterward, have them discuss the mentoring experience and the effectiveness of their methods.	
Behavior	Have students think of someone less experienced than themselves in their major, club, organization, or workplace who may benefit from having a mentor. Encourage each of the students to develop a relationship with that person and see if it becomes a mentoring relationship.	Productive Relationships

Motivation

There are many factors that can influence someone's motivation to complete a task or goal. Some people may be motivated by internal factors such as drive and desire, whereas others may be motivated by external factors like rewards and incentives. It is essential for the leader to understand the unique ways in which people are motivated and engage in specific strategies that motivate each person in the way that is most effective for him or her.

The Spirit Club has one week to hand-make two thousand pom-poms to give away at homecoming. Even if everyone in the organization helped make them, it would still be a lot of work. Knowing this, the executive board asks each member what a good incentive would be for each person who made fifty pom-poms. They post online all of the incentive ideas that are feasible for the organization to offer. Some ideas include a coffee coupon, movie tickets, and name in the semester newsletter. Every member of the organization then selects for themselves which incentive they want to make fifty pom-poms.

Motivation Competencies
Understands how to motivate others (Knowledge):
Understanding a variety of motivation strategies and how to select and apply motivation strategies specific to each person.

Values motivating others (Value):
Believing that it is important to select and apply motivation strategies specific to each person in an effort to best inspire and encourage that person to complete a task or achieve a goal.

Has skills to motivate others (Ability):
Being able to select and apply motivation strategies specific to each person.

Motivates others (Behavior):
Selecting and applying motivation strategies specific to each person.

Related Competency Areas
- Mentoring
- Empowerment
- Excellence

CAS Domain Translation
- Interpersonal Competence

Leadership Model Translation
- Relational Leadership Model: Empowering
- Five Practices of Exemplary Leadership: Enable Others to Act; Encourage the Heart
- Emotionally Intelligent Leadership: Inspiration

Motivation Curricular Ideas

Dimension(s)	Curriculum	Other Competency Areas Developed
Knowledge	Have students list what motivates them. Have them share this insight with others and learn how people are motivated differently.	
Knowledge	Have students brainstorm ways that they could learn how others like to be motivated.	
Value	Ask students to reflect on a time that someone tried to motivate them but used a strategy that didn't match how they like to be motivated. Have them discuss the impact of that experience and what strategy would have worked best in that context.	
Ability	Have students ask others in their organization how they like to be motivated and create an organizational motivation chart for everyone to see what motivates each member.	
Ability	Give students a case study in which an organization is planning a group project. Then, give them five different motivation strategies and have them apply each one to the case. How would each be implemented and what are the pros and cons of each strategy in that context?	Evaluation
Behavior	Have students pair up and give them a task. Have one student use different strategies to motivate the other student to complete the task.	

Others' Contributions

Leaders know that the unique ideas, strengths, knowledge, and abilities that individuals bring to a task or relationship are assets, because no one person has every great idea or a mastery of all competencies, and certainly leaders cannot do it all alone. Leaders understand this and integrate others' ideas, strengths, and abilities to better address an issue, strengthen a relationship, solve a problem, or engage in innovation.

Polly is working on a semester-long group project with Sam and Wes. The project involves them investigating a community issue, writing a paper with their recommendations to address the issue, and then doing a ten-minute presentation to the community members affected by the issue. Polly comes to the group already knowing that she is going to take charge and probably be the one to put together both the paper and presentation because that seems to always be her role. After she starts meeting with the group, she learns that Wes is a journalism major and is a fantastic writer and that Sam has a tech background and can design a really professional presentation that integrates videos and exciting content. Polly is used to being the one to do these aspects of group work, but she is pleased to learn of the strengths of her group members and is excited for them to do these roles. Polly found that by having Sam and Wes do the tasks related to their strengths, not only is the end product going to be better, but she is freed up to engage in researching the issue which is her favorite part of group projects.

Others' Contributions Competencies
Understands how to utilize others' contributions effectively (Knowledge):
Understanding how to utilize others' ideas, strengths, knowledge, and abilities so that each person is operating at his or her highest capacity both for the success and morale of each individual as well as higher productivity and effectiveness of the group; understanding how to put the right people in the right places.

Values utilizing others' contributions effectively (Value):
Believing that others' ideas, strengths, knowledge, and abilities are valuable and that by utilizing their assets in an effective manner, each person can operate at his or her highest capacity both for the success and morale of each individual as well as higher productivity and effectiveness of the group.

Has skills to utilize others' contributions effectively (Ability):
Being able to utilize others' ideas, strengths, knowledge, and abilities so that each person is operating at his or her highest capacity both for the success and morale of each individual as well as higher productivity and effectiveness of the group; being able to put the right people in the right places.

Utilizes others' contributions effectively (Behavior):
Utilizing others' ideas, strengths, knowledge, and abilities so that each person is operating at his or her highest capacity both for the success and morale of each individual as well as higher productivity and effectiveness of the group; putting the right people in the right places.

Related Competency Areas

- Other Perspectives
- Scope of Competence
- Receiving Feedback

CAS Domain Translation

- Interpersonal Competence

Leadership Model Translation

- Relational Leadership Model: Empowering; Inclusive
- Social Change Model of Leadership: Collaboration
- Five Practices of Exemplary Leadership: Enable Others to Act
- Emotionally Intelligent Leadership: Capitalizing on Difference; Coaching

Others' Contributions Curricular Ideas

Dimension(s)	Curriculum	Other Competency Areas Developed
Knowledge	Give students a problem to solve and have them come up with all the competencies that would be helpful for the group to have to most effectively solve the problem. How can they engage each person to contribute to their fullest to best solve the problem?	Problem Solving
Value	Have students discuss a time when they knew that they were exactly right for a role they were in, given their strengths, abilities, assets, and so on. What was the situation and how did it feel to be a good fit?	
Value	Have students share a time when they experienced being mismatched for a role based on their strengths, abilities, assets, and so on or witnessed someone else mismatched for a role. Why was there a mismatch? How did that affect others and the task at hand?	
Value	Ask students to brainstorm situations in which utilizing others' strengths, abilities, assets, and so on could be beneficial to group functioning.	

Others' Contributions Curricular Ideas

Dimension(s)	Curriculum	Other Competency Areas Developed
Ability	Give students a scenario in which they are the president of an organization and have the chance to appoint four people to their cabinet. Describe each of the cabinet roles. Share descriptions of four people and have the students place each person in the role best suited for that person based on his or her strengths, abilities, assets, and so on.	Analysis Evaluation
Behavior	Have students engage in assessing the strengths, abilities, assets, and so on of a group they are working with on a task or project. Then, have them assess whether they have the right people in the right roles. If they do not, have them move roles and duties around so that each person is the best match with what they can contribute.	Evaluation Decision Making

Empowerment

Leaders understand the benefit of empowering others. Sharing power, information, and resources allows others to have an investment in a task or process and can provide them a sense of ownership, accountability, and commitment. This may lead to higher-quality work, greater timeliness and follow-through, and greater commitment to the task and team.

The Physiology Student Association (PSA) is very well known for the large number of volunteers who assist at free health clinics in the community. Lately, however, it appears that the clinics need resources such as medical supplies rather than volunteer time. So, the president of PSA, Shelly, asks every person in the organization to write down one idea to address the issue of the increased need in clinic supplies. She then reads each idea aloud at the next meeting, getting feedback from all of the members. The group decides on three ideas and forms three committees, each focusing on one idea. Although Shelly knows the stakes are high and that she has a tendency to run most of these kinds of initiatives herself, she asks for volunteers to chair each of the three committees. She then asks the committee chairs and their members to spend the entire time for the next two meetings creating a strategic plan to initiate the idea they are charged with. She knows that it is important for all members of the committees to be involved in this process and certainly for the chairs to take ownership over the group process if they are to be successful and have a commitment from everyone.

Empowerment Competencies

Understands how to empower others (Knowledge):

Understanding strategies to share power, information, and resources with others so they can have a sense of ownership, accountability, and commitment regarding a task or process.

Values empowering others (Value):

Believing that it is important to share power, information, and resources with others so they can have a sense of ownership, accountability, and commitment regarding a task or process so as to lead to higher-quality work, greater timeliness and follow-through, and greater commitment to the task and team.

Has skills to empower others (Ability):

Being able to share power, information, and resources with others so they can have a sense of ownership, accountability, and commitment regarding a task or process.

Empowers others (Behavior):

Sharing power, information, and resources with others so they can have a sense of ownership, accountability, and commitment regarding a task or process.

Related Competency Areas

- Mentoring
- Motivation
- Supervision
- Power Dynamics

CAS Domain Translation

- Interpersonal Competence

Leadership Model Translation

- Relational Leadership Model: Empowering
- Social Change Model of Leadership: Collaboration
- Five Practices of Exemplary Leadership: Enable Others to Act
- Emotionally Intelligent Leadership: Developing Others; Coaching

Empowerment Curricular Ideas

Dimension(s)	Curriculum	Other Competency Areas Developed
Knowledge	Share with students strategies they can use to empower others.	
Knowledge	Have students reflect on what power they have in a group or organization, consider what they already do that is empowering and what they might do better to empower others.	Reflection and Application Power Dynamics
Value	Have students discuss the pros and cons of empowerment, focusing on what holds people back from empowering others.	
Ability	Have students analyze a case study in which they identify strategies that can be used to empower certain characters in the case study.	Analysis
Behavior	Have students who are in a position of power in a club, job, organization, and so on empower someone regarding a task or process. Then, have the students discuss what it was like to engage in empowerment, what hesitancies, if any, they had in empowering another person, and what transpired from the situation.	

Providing Feedback

Feedback includes critiques, confirmations, and/or advice that can help another person improve their decisions, effectiveness, productivity, or interactions with others. As a leader, being able to provide feedback to others is essential. This feedback not only assists the one receiving the feedback, but if the feedback that is given is utilized, this can have a positive impact on group functioning and group productivity.

The Campus Cleanup Crew is a very active organization and is dedicated to keeping the campus clean and free from litter. Each month, the crew gets together and divides into four task forces that engage in a different cleanup project for that month. Members volunteer for whichever task force they are most interested in, so most students end up working with each other during the course of the semester. Juan, the president, has noticed that most individuals will wait until a particular member, Arielle, has selected

(Continued)

which task force she wants to be on before selecting one themselves so they don't have to be on a task force with her. He knows it is because Arielle complains a lot, and the task forces she is on often end up being difficult for others to be on. Juan decides to discuss this with Arielle before the selection of the next task forces. During the discussion, Juan asks Arielle how her experience has been on the task forces and then proceeds to share with her the effect her complaining is having on the group. Arielle is shocked to find this out because she thought she was just kidding around, not really complaining. She is somewhat embarrassed by this and changes her behavior for future crew meetings and events.

Providing Feedback Competencies

Understands how to provide feedback to others effectively (Knowledge):

Understanding strategies to offer critiques, confirmations, and/or advice in a manner that is timely and respectful in an effort to improve another person's decisions, effectiveness, productivity, or interactions with others.

Values providing feedback to others effectively (Value):

Believing that it is important to offer critiques, confirmations, and/or advice in a manner that is timely and respectful in an effort to improve another person's decisions, effectiveness, productivity, or interactions with others.

Has skills to provide feedback to others effectively (Ability):

Being able to offer critiques, confirmations, and/or advice in a manner that is timely and respectful in an effort to improve another person's decisions, effectiveness, productivity, or interactions with others.

Provides feedback to others effectively (Behavior):

Offering critiques, confirmations, and/or advice in a manner that is timely and respectful in an effort to improve another person's decisions, effectiveness, productivity, or interactions with others.

Related Competency Areas

- Mentoring
- Empowerment
- Supervision
- Verbal Communication

CAS Domain Translation

- Interpersonal Competence

Leadership Model Translation

- Relational Leadership Model: Process-Oriented
- Social Change Model of Leadership: Controversy with Civility
- Five Practices of Exemplary Leadership: Enable Others to Act
- Emotionally Intelligent Leadership: Coaching

Providing Feedback Curricular Ideas

Dimension(s)	Curriculum	Other Competency Areas Developed
Knowledge	Share with students effective strategies to give feedback that is specific and delivered in a respectful manner.	
Knowledge	Have students reflect on feedback they received from someone else that was delivered in an effective manner. Have students work together to create a list that captures all the strategies that they experienced that were effective in providing feedback to them.	Reflection and Application
Value	Have students discuss the importance of giving feedback to others and the implication of not giving feedback.	
Value	Have students think about how they give feedback (if they do, the frequency, the timeliness, and the specificity) and what influences them to give feedback in this manner.	
Ability	Have students analyze a case study in which a person is demonstrating a behavior that needs to be addressed. Have the students work together to determine the best way to give that person feedback and what feedback should be given.	Analysis
Ability	Have students engage in a role play to practice giving feedback to one another. Each person can take on a character so the role play has a context in which the feedback is appropriate. Have the students share what the experience of giving feedback was like and have them critique each other's feedback delivery.	
Ability Behavior	Have students think of someone that they would like to give feedback to (critique, confirmation, or advice). Have them brainstorm strategies to most effectively give this feedback. Then have them give the feedback (if it is timely and appropriate) and reflect on how that experience was.	

Supervision

In many cases, leaders oversee the work of others, whether formally or informally. Thus, it is essential that leaders are able to effectively provide direction to those they supervise so they are clear about what they need to do, the process for doing it, and any expectations the leader has. This direction can provide a sense of clarity and transparency so that others are best situated to complete their intended jobs or tasks.

Stacy is the student lead for the information desk at the student union and oversees twelve student staff members. Stacy notices that most of her employees are very effective; they have great customer service and perform job functions well. She has two employees, Jimmy and Anne, though, who both have inadequate customer service skills. Jimmy is very knowledgeable about campus and can answer just about any question, as long as he looks up from his homework long enough to do so. Anne is very friendly but just does not know campus at all. She often answers questions with "I don't know." Stacy knows that both of these employees need good supervision so they can be more effective in their roles. For Jimmy, Stacy realizes that the best approach is to discuss the expectations of the job and ask why he is buried in his homework instead of helping others. From this conversation, Stacy learns that Jimmy's work schedule is so spread out that he has few substantial blocks of study time. She decides to change his work schedule to be more compatible with studying but lets him know that he will need to put customers before his homework and that when someone asks a question, he will need to look up from his studying and give that person his full attention. For Anne, Stacy decides the best course of action is twofold: Anne will study campus resources during down times at work and she will shadow more seasoned workers. This helps Anne be more effective, and with Stacy's checking in, she is getting the direction she needs to be successful.

Supervision Competencies
Understands how to supervise others effectively (Knowledge):
Understanding strategies to provide direction to supervisees so they are clear about what they need to do, the process for doing it, and any expectations the leader has.

Values supervising others effectively (Value):
Believing that if supervisees are going to best complete their intended jobs or tasks it is important to provide direction so they are clear about what they need to do, the process for doing it, and any expectations the leader has.

Has skills to supervise others effectively (Ability):

Being able to provide direction to supervisees so they are clear about what they need to do, the process for doing it, and any expectations the leader has.

Supervises others effectively (Behavior):

Providing direction to supervisees so they are clear about what they need to do, the process for doing it, and any expectations the leader has.

Related Competency Areas

- Receiving Feedback
- Mentoring
- Motivation
- Others' Contributions
- Empowerment
- Providing Feedback
- Others' Circumstances

CAS Domain Translation

- Interpersonal Competence

Leadership Model Translation

- Relational Leadership Model: Empowering; Process-Oriented
- Five Practices of Exemplary Leadership: Enable Others to Act
- Emotionally Intelligent Leadership: Coaching

Supervision Curricular Ideas

Dimension(s)	Curriculum	Other Competency Areas Developed
Knowledge	Have students discuss attributes of their best supervisors and their worst supervisors. Then, have them reflect on how they could use lessons learned about what to do and what not to do when they supervise.	Reflection and Application
Knowledge	Share with students concepts related to situational leadership and adapting one's leadership style to different people and situations.	Appropriate Interaction

(Continued)

Supervision Curricular Ideas (Continued)

Dimension(s)	Curriculum	Other Competency Areas Developed
Value	Have students discuss a time that they oversaw the work of others. How did the direction they provided affect the person's ability to complete the job or task to the best of their ability? Should they have provided more direction? Less direction?	
Ability	Have students analyze a case study about an employee who is struggling on the job. Ask the students what strategies the supervisor should employ to assist that employee in succeeding.	Analysis Problem Solving
Ability	Have students develop an action plan of how they can develop attributes of an effective supervisor.	Plan
Behavior	If students are involved in a leadership role in either volunteer or employment experiences, have them ask those whom they oversee to fill out an evaluation (anonymous or not) about their supervisory skills. Then, have the students create a plan to address any challenges that arose in the evaluations.	Receiving Feedback

Collaboration

There are a variety of situations in which it is more beneficial to work together than to work independently. These may include solving a challenging problem, addressing an ethical dilemma, or simply completing a comprehensive project. Being able to work together allows a multitude of voices and ideas to be considered, an enhanced sense of group commitment and responsibility to occur, and the human power to execute a task to increase. Leaders foster a culture of collaboration and seek to bring people together in intentional ways to benefit the group.

The Delta fraternity is very committed to philanthropy and wants to raise $50,000 for cancer research. But, there are only thirty-five members in the fraternity, and they cannot conceptualize what they could do with only thirty-five people to raise that amount of money. So, they decide to approach the Chi fraternity and ask whether they would like to work together on this initiative. The Chi fraternity immediately jumps on, along with six other fraternities. Representatives from each fraternity come together to discuss ideas to raise the $50,000. They agree on having a 5K race in the community. For an entire semester, the members of all eight fraternities work together to plan logistics, design marketing, and get sponsorships. The 5K ends up bringing in $62,000 thanks to the group effort.

Collaboration Competencies
Understands how to collaborate effectively (Knowledge):
Understanding strategies to work with others toward a common objective through the sharing of ideas and distribution of responsibilities across team members.

Values collaborating effectively (Value):
Believing that it is important to work with others toward a common objective through the sharing of ideas and distribution of responsibilities across team members in an effort to reach the objective most effectively.

Has skills to collaborate effectively (Ability):
Being able to work with others toward a common objective through the sharing of ideas and distribution of responsibilities across team members.

Collaborates effectively (Behavior):
Working with others toward a common objective through the sharing of ideas and distribution of responsibilities across team members.

Related Competency Areas
- Productive Relationships
- Motivation
- Empowerment
- Group Development
- Listening
- Excellence

CAS Domain Translation
- Interpersonal Competence

Leadership Model Translation

- Relational Leadership Model: Process-Oriented
- Social Change Model of Leadership: Collaboration
- Five Practices of Exemplary Leadership: Enable Others to Act
- Emotionally Intelligent Leadership: Teamwork

Collaboration Curricular Ideas

Dimension(s)	Curriculum	Other Competency Areas Developed
Knowledge	Have students discuss strategies for effective collaboration.	
Knowledge	Have students discuss a team that they have been on that collaborated effectively and describe to the others what behaviors the team members engaged in that made the collaboration effective.	
Value	Have students brainstorm effects of not collaborating when in groups or teams.	
Ability	Give students a task to practice collaboration. Have them reflect on how well they think they collaborated.	
Behavior	Have students collaborate on something (project, decision, initiative, and so on) in their day-to-day lives using effective collaboration strategies. Then, have them share with the group how well they think they used the strategies.	Evaluation

Chapter 4

Group Dynamics

Organizational Behavior

Organizations can be living entities, with the organization and its individuals creating and sustaining their own sense of culture, norms, and practices. Leaders need to understand the organization and also to anticipate, navigate, mitigate, and respond effectively to the behaviors of the organization and those in it to lead most effectively in the organizational context.

Sarah was recently elected as student body president. Except for Sarah, members of the executive board have had extensive involvement in student government. For her first executive board meeting, Sarah prepares by setting an agenda and putting name plates for each board member at an assigned seat. When the board members arrive, they appear a little taken aback, but nonetheless sit down at their assigned seats. As Sarah moves through the agenda, members of the board don't speak up. After the meeting, the group begins chatting and joking with each other as they appear to head out to dinner together, without Sarah. Sarah begins to realize that she has not been part of this organization and needs to understand the culture of the organization and how the members interact. So, for the next meeting, she doesn't create an agenda or put out name plates but asks everyone to share what they like about being on student government. Through this process, she realizes that what most people enjoy is creating the meeting agenda together and having a more informal environment. Sarah then begins working with the board each week to develop the agenda, and the meetings are a lot less formal. After the very next meeting, the group asks Sarah to join them for dinner.

Organizational Behavior Competencies
Understands organizational behavior (Knowledge):
Understanding the ways in which individuals and groups behave toward each other and the organization and how this behavior affects the organization.

Values understanding organizational behavior (Value):

Believing that it is important to understand behaviors of individuals and groups and their impact on an organization in an effort to more effectively navigate the organization.

Has skills to respond to organizational behavior effectively (Ability):

Being able to make meaning of individual and group behaviors and their impact within an organization so as to effectively navigate the organization.

Responds to organizational behavior effectively (Behavior):

Making meaning of individual and group behaviors and their impact within an organization and then using this understanding to effectively navigate the organization.

Related Competency Areas

- Analysis
- Evaluation
- Decision Making

CAS Domain Translation

- Cognitive Complexity

Leadership Model Translation

- Relational Leadership Model: Process-Oriented
- Social Change Model of Leadership: Common Purpose
- Emotionally Intelligent Leadership: Group Savvy

Organizational Behavior Curricular Ideas

Dimension(s)	Curriculum	Other Competency Areas Developed
Knowledge	Share with students concepts such as culture, norms, practices, and rituals as they relate to organizational behavior.	
Value	Have students discuss a time that it was valuable for them as group members to understand the organizational behavior of their group. How was it valuable?	
Ability	Have students develop a plan to more effectively navigate their organizations given the behaviors of individuals and groups within the organizations.	Plan

Organizational Behavior Curricular Ideas

Dimension(s)	Curriculum	Other Competency Areas Developed
Ability	Have students describe their ideal organization and brainstorm ways to shape the behaviors of individuals and groups to result in this ideal organization.	Idea Generation
Ability	Have students reflect on what actions they take to attempt to navigate an organization they belong to.	
Behavior	Have the students do a culture audit of another organization, department, or office by observing people's interactions, processes, and practices. Then, have them report back their observations on culture, norms, practices, and rituals.	Analysis
Behavior	Have students assess their own organizations and interpret how the behaviors of individuals and groups within the organization are affecting the organization.	Analysis Evaluation
Behavior	Have students discuss with others in their organizations how their behaviors contribute to the culture, norms, practices, and rituals of the organization. What meaning might an outsider associate with their behaviors?	Analysis

Power Dynamics

Whether formal or informal, internal and external power dynamics affect nearly every group. These power dynamics may be influenced by position, seniority, resource access, and/or relationships of the group's members or stakeholders. It is vital that leaders understand the types of power dynamics that exist in their groups so they can better respond to the group's needs within the context of these power dynamics.

Pete is the newly elected president of the Honor Board, the peer judicial board that all academic integrity violations are referred to for hearings and sanctioning. The Honor Board is the campus's oldest student organization, having been around for nearly seventy-five years, and since its inception, the Honor Board has never accepted anyone with a class standing below a junior. For the past several years, first- and second-year students, along with members of other organizations, have been lobbying the Honor Board to extend its membership to second-year students to create fairer representation of the campus community, especially since most students referred to an Honor Board hearing are first and second year. In an attempt to change this policy, Pete knows he has to carefully navigate the power dynamics internal and external

(Continued)

to the group, including the juniors and seniors who had to wait until they were third-year students to join. Then, there is Riley, the organization's oldest member, who some refer to as the grandparent of the organization because he is a graduate student who has served on the board for three years. People love Riley and respect his ideas. He will have influence based on what he believes. Finally, there are the alumni. Past members of the Honor Board are some of the biggest donors to the school. The vice president of the Honor Board, Sandra, supports the change and works closely with staff and faculty members across campus who have indicated that they support the change. Pete decides his best course of action is to work with Riley because he knows that Riley's voice is much stronger than anyone else's in the organization or any of the faculty or staff. He also plans to reach out to some interested alumni to get them involved in the process. This is a sensitive subject, and Pete wants to make sure he approaches it in the best manner possible.

Power Dynamics Competencies
Understands power dynamics (Knowledge):
Understanding what power dynamics may look like, the impact of power dynamics, and how to respond to power dynamics effectively in a group or organization.

Values understanding power dynamics (Value):
Believing that it is important to understand that there are internal and external power dynamics that affect nearly all groups and organizations; understanding what power dynamics may look like, the impact of power dynamics, and how to respond to power dynamics effectively can be beneficial in responding to power dynamics in a group or organization.

Has skills to respond to power dynamics effectively (Ability):
Being able to identify the internal and external power dynamics that affect a group or organization and to use that knowledge to respond to them effectively.

Responds to power dynamics effectively (Behavior):
Identifying and effectively responding to the internal and external power dynamics that affect a group or organization.

Related Competency Areas

- Decision Making
- Appropriate Interaction
- Empowerment
- Organizational Behavior

CAS Domain Translation

- Cognitive Complexity

Leadership Model Translation

- Relational Leadership Model: Empowering
- Emotionally Intelligent Leadership: Group Savvy

Power Dynamics Curricular Ideas

Dimension(s)	Curriculum	Other Competency Areas Developed
Knowledge	Share what power dynamics might look like and how to effectively identify them in a group or organization.	
Knowledge	Have students share ways they have effectively responded to power dynamics.	
Value	Have students discuss a time that understanding power dynamics internal and external to their group was beneficial. What was the situation? What was the impact of the power dynamics on the group?	
Ability	Have students brainstorm internal and external power dynamics that may affect an organization they belong to.	
Ability	Have students create an organization web laying out all the formal and informal power relationships of members in the group. Then, have them explore what factors of those relationships are power laden and how one can navigate those power structures.	Analysis
Ability	Have students role-play a politicking scenario in which they have to attempt to achieve a goal by navigating the power structures present in the scenario.	
Ability	Have students read about a current event. Ask them to discuss all the power structures present in the situation and how those structures may affect the behaviors of individuals and the outcome of the situation. Have them suggest a course of action to address the situation that takes into account the power structures.	Analysis
Ability Behavior	Have students reflect on a situation in their organization that is affected by internal or external power. Have them come up with a plan of action to effectively navigate the power dynamics. If they are able to, have them attempt to implement their plan in their organization and report the outcome back to the group.	Analysis Plan

Group Development

Working together is not just about achieving an outcome; it is about participating in a process. Leaders need to pay attention to the group process, ensuring that the group feels a sense of connection and commitment to both the group and to its members. This connection and commitment can foster a sense of trust through which members share ideas, give feedback, follow through, and make difficult decisions. By understanding how groups form and develop, the leader can help foster group development and thus enhance the group's efficiency and effectiveness in an empowering manner.

Tia is chair of the Family Weekend Planning Committee. There are ten other students on this committee, all focused on the planning and coordination of Family Weekend events such as the faculty meet-and-greet as well as the family barbecue. Each committee member has a specific role, whether that is marketing, logistics, outreach, or finance. Although their roles are specific, each member relies heavily on the completion of tasks of others because many of their functions are interrelated (for example, outreach cannot begin to outreach unless marketing designs and prints materials). Because of this, it is essential that the group functions well together. Tia knows that if the group is not on the same page, not only will tasks not get done but interpersonal issues may emerge in the group. So, Tia decides that the first thing that the group is going to do is to have a team-building day. She arranges for the group to be together the entire day learning about each other and how best to work together. Once a month, Tia designates the entire meeting to group check-in and team building to enhance the group process and ensure the highest level of group functioning.

Group Development Competencies

Understands how to facilitate the process of group development (Knowledge):

Understanding strategies to assist groups in developing a sense of shared purpose, commitment, trust, and effectiveness.

Values facilitating the process of group development (Value):

Believing that it is important to assist groups in developing a sense of shared purpose, commitment, trust, and effectiveness so that group members work together in the most effective, efficient, and empowering manner.

Has skills to facilitate the process of group development (Ability):

Being able to assist groups in developing a sense of shared purpose, commitment, trust, and effectiveness.

Facilitates the process of group development (Behavior):

Assisting groups in developing a sense of shared purpose, commitment, trust, and effectiveness.

Related Competency Areas

- Empowerment
- Collaboration
- Excellence

CAS Domain Translation

- Interpersonal Competence

Leadership Model Translation

- Relational Leadership Model: Process-Oriented
- Social Change Model of Leadership: Common Purpose; Collaboration
- Five Practices of Exemplary Leadership: Enable Others to Act; Inspire a Shared Vision
- Emotionally Intelligent Leadership: Teamwork; Group Savvy

Group Development Curricular Ideas

Dimension(s)	Curriculum	Other Competency Areas Developed
Knowledge	Brainstorm with students strategies to develop a shared purpose, commitment, trust, and effectiveness within groups.	
Knowledge	Explain how to use theories and models of group development.	
Knowledge	Have students reflect on a group that has a high sense of shared purpose, commitment, trust, and effectiveness and have them recount what it was about the group that fostered these characteristics.	
Value	Have students discuss the benefits of being in a group with a high sense of shared purpose, commitment, trust, and effectiveness. Have them discuss the drawbacks of groups that don't have these characteristics.	
Ability	Have students create an action plan for a group they are in that outlines strategies to develop the group into one with a high sense of shared purpose, commitment, trust, and effectiveness.	Plan
Behavior	Have students participate in a team-building experience as a group. Process the activity by asking students to share their thoughts on the group process and how the activities affected group functioning.	Collaboration
Behavior	Have students create a list of community standards (mutual expectations of each other) for their organizations.	

Creating Change

Nothing stays the same; people change, environments change, and organizations change. Not only is change inevitable, it can be challenging for people, structures, and processes. And, if change is not instituted well, it can be damaging to the group and its members. Thus, it is imperative that when leaders enact change, they are sensitive to the context and people involved.

It appears to Jess and everyone else that the selection process in place for interviewing new members for the senior honorary is tedious, drawn out, complex, and time consuming, both for the interviewers and interviewees. Everyone in the organization agrees that something needs to change. With applications going out in two weeks, Jess knows that a change needs to happen now for it to be implemented this cycle. So, Jess decides it's time to make a change, one that is sustainable, manageable, and that everyone can agree on. Jess gives the group some parameters, such as that the process cannot take up more than one weekend day, it must be completed before a certain date, and more than one person must have interacted with each applicant. She then asks each person to put together a proposal for how a more effective selection process could look. She asks for the proposals to address the specifics of what each group member would like to see changed in the selection process. She also asks them to outline the internal and external impact their proposed change would have and how this change should best be implemented given the context and culture of the organization. At the next meeting, Jess has each member give a two-minute overview of his or her proposal. Jess leads the group through a discussion about elements of each proposal, along with the pros and cons. After analyzing the various ideas, the group comes to an agreement about the new selection process that fits with the needs of the organization as well as positively affects members of the organization. They further lay out an implementation process, decide who will be involved in the change, and determine how they plan to evaluate the new process.

Creating Change Competencies
Understands how to create change effectively (Knowledge):
Understanding how to apply strategies that are both appropriate and within the context at hand in order to create change on a group, organizational, and/or societal level.

Values creating change effectively (Value):
Believing that it is important to use the most appropriate methods of creating change given each situation's context in order to create change on a group, organizational, and/or societal level.

Has skills to create change effectively (Ability):

Being able to apply strategies that are both appropriate and within the context at hand in order to create change on a group, organizational, and/or societal level.

Creates change effectively (Behavior):

Using the most appropriate methods of creating change given each situation's context in order to create change on a group, organizational, and/or societal level.

Related Competency Areas

- Evaluation
- Decision Making
- Empathy
- Organizational Behavior

CAS Domain Translation

- Cognitive Complexity

Leadership Model Translation

- Relational Leadership Model: Purposeful; Process-Oriented
- Social Change Model of Leadership: Change
- Five Practices of Exemplary Leadership: Challenge the Process
- Emotionally Intelligent Leadership: Change Agent

Creating Change Curricular Ideas

Dimension(s)	Curriculum	Other Competency Areas Developed
Knowledge	Have students identify a change they have been affected by. Have them analyze the strategies used to create the change. What strategies worked well? What could have been done differently?	Analysis Evaluation
Value	Have students reflect on a change they were involved in creating. Have them assess how sustainable that change has been and how much support from others that change has had. Have them think about what they might do now (after this change was enacted) to continue to increase its sustainability and support.	Evaluation

Creating Change Curricular Ideas (Continued)

Dimension(s)	Curriculum	Other Competency Areas Developed
Ability	Give students a case study about a change that needs to be implemented in an organization. Have them come up with the strategy to most effectively implement that change.	Analysis
Behavior	Have students identify a change they would like to make in a group or organization. After having them lay out a plan, have them try to implement that change. Then, have them report back to the group about their experience in doing this.	Plan
Behavior	Have students come up with an issue in a group or organization they belong to. Have them lead a conversation with this group or organization about what could be changed to address the issue, keeping in mind context, sustainability, and impact of the change on others.	

Chapter 5

Civic Responsibility

Diversity

Leadership is inherently an interpersonal process, and in many situations, leaders will find themselves in the position of working with individuals who have different backgrounds, beliefs, and/or experiences than they do. The variety of diverse perspectives of those in the group can enhance a group's effectiveness. Instead of a decision being made from only one or maybe two vantage points, differing perspectives can be considered and integrated into the decision. This allows for a decision to not only be more comprehensive but also more inclusive. In addition, diversity can enhance group functioning because individuals are exposed to people with backgrounds, beliefs, and/or experiences that are different than theirs and are able to challenge stereotypes that impede effective and productive relationships.

Jasmine is on the programming committee for the Campus Health and Wellness Team. The committee's job is to put on a variety of health and wellness awareness programs for the entire student body. In an effort to address the health and wellness needs of the campus community, the committee must be able to tap into the diversity of the committee when planning programs. Thus, each year, the committee is very conscientious about recruiting a diverse committee (backgrounds, beliefs, experiences, and so on) so that multiple perspectives are considered when developing programs that meet the needs of a variety of individuals. In addition, the committee forms formal partnerships with a variety of campus groups, including the Veterans Center; Commuter Student Association; Graduate Student Government; the Intercultural Greek Council; the Interfaith Association; Women's Resource Center; the Lesbian, Gay, Bisexual Student Association; and many others. The diversity on the committee and these partnerships are invaluable for the committee's ability to ensure that programming on health and wellness is as comprehensive and inclusive to the needs of as many as possible.

Diversity Competencies
Understands the value of diversity (Knowledge):
Understanding the importance of having exposure to people from different backgrounds, beliefs, and/or experiences.

Values diversity (Value):
Believing that having exposure to people from different backgrounds, beliefs, and/or experiences can be valuable in enhancing group effectiveness and group functioning.

Motivated to promote diversity (Ability):
Being motivated to actively promote one's own and/or others' exposure to people from a variety of backgrounds, beliefs, and/or experiences, in an effort to enhance group effectiveness and/or group functioning.

Promotes diversity (Behavior):
Promoting one's own and/or others' exposure to people from a variety of backgrounds, beliefs, and/or experiences to enhance group effectiveness and/or group functioning.

Related Competency Areas
- Other Perspectives
- Productive Relationships
- Others' Contributions
- Others' Circumstances
- Inclusion

CAS Domain Translation
- Humanitarianism and Civic Engagement

Leadership Model Translation
- Relational Leadership Model: Inclusive
- Social Change Model of Leadership: Controversy with Civility
- Emotionally Intelligent Leadership: Capitalizing on Difference

Diversity Curricular Ideas

Dimension(s)	Curriculum	Other Competency Areas Developed
Knowledge	Have students reflect on what groups of people they are not exposed to often and why. Then, have them brainstorm ways to increase their exposure to people who are different than they are.	
Knowledge	Have students think about their five closest friends. Have them assess how similar or different they are to each of these friends, considering factors such as race, class, gender, religion, sexual orientation, ability, major, political affiliation, and so on.	Analysis Evaluation
Value	Have students share an experience when being in a diverse group was valuable.	
Ability	Have students review their marketing, programming, and recruitment processes of an organization they are in to see how the organization is appealing to a representative group of individuals reflective of campus demographics and then brainstorm ways to increase this scope, if necessary.	Analysis
Behavior	Have students interview someone with at least one different identity than them (race, gender, sexual orientation, religion, and so on). Have them ask for general information about that identity as well as about the person's own experience.	Other Perspectives Verbal Communication Listening
Behavior	Have students attend an event that will expose them to people who are different than they are.	

Others' Circumstances

It is critical for leaders to seek to understand the situations and/or conditions of other people. This understanding not only helps inform the leader's decisions but also helps the leader be conscious of what others have experienced or are experiencing so as to engage in inclusive behaviors and connect with others with a sense of care.

Jim is in a study group for one of his classes and often finds himself in the position of scheduling the sessions and informing everyone of when and where they are meeting. In his planning, he is intentional in picking locations that are located close to a bus line so that the two members without cars can easily access the study sessions. Jim also knows that some of the group members have children and many work in addition to taking classes, so he schedules the sessions using an online program that allows group members to indicate the times they are available.

Others' Circumstances Competencies

Understands others' circumstances (Knowledge):

Understanding the conditions and/or situations of other individuals and/or groups.

Values understanding others' circumstances (Value):

Believing that it is important to understand the conditions and/or situations of other individuals and/or groups so as to integrate this understanding into one's behaviors to be inclusive and demonstrate a sense of care.

Motivated to respond appropriately to others' circumstances (Ability):

Being motivated to integrate an understanding of the conditions and/or situations of other individuals and/or groups into one's behaviors to be inclusive and demonstrate a sense of care.

Responds appropriately to others' circumstances (Behavior):

Integrating an understanding of the conditions and/or situations of other individuals and/or groups into one's behaviors to be inclusive and demonstrate a sense of care.

Related Competency Areas

- Other Perspectives
- Productive Relationships
- Appropriate Interaction
- Empathy
- Diversity
- Inclusion
- Listening

CAS Domain Translation

- Humanitarianism and Civic Engagement

Leadership Model Translation

- Relational Leadership Model: Inclusive
- Social Change Model: Controversy with Civility
- Five Practices of Exemplary Leadership: Encourage the Heart
- Emotionally Intelligent Leadership: Empathy

Others' Circumstances Curricular Ideas

Dimension(s)	Curriculum	Other Competency Areas Developed
Knowledge	Give students opportunities to hear speakers from a variety of backgrounds so that they can develop an understanding of the speakers' circumstances and how those circumstances affect their lives. This can also be done through watching documentaries or reading memoirs.	
Value	Have students reflect on and discuss their own circumstances and how others have or have not appropriately responded to those circumstances.	
Ability	Have students analyze two or more case studies in which the only differences are of the personal circumstances of the characters in the studies. Have them think about how these differences in personal circumstances affect the situations of the characters.	Analysis
Behavior	Have students assume leadership roles that will require them to consider the circumstances of various individuals or groups in decision making, such as roles in marketing, programming, or recruitment for their organization.	
Behavior	Have students engage in service learning projects that expose them to groups with whom they have not previously interacted, including an opportunity for intentional reflection before, during, and after the projects.	Reflection and Application Service

Inclusion

Leaders do not just lead abstract groups of people for abstract causes; they lead with people and for people. Because people like to feel included, whether to share their viewpoints, contribute to a cause or task, or simply feel a sense of belonging, leaders must foster an inclusive environment.

Teresa is chair of the social committee for the Union Programming Board (UPB). Each year, the UPB puts on a holiday celebration right before final exam time in the winter so that everyone can come to a study break and celebrate Christmas. Teresa knows that having a social and study break is great for this time of year, but she is aware that centering the theme around Christmas is not inclusive of all students. So, Teresa and the committee decide to change the theme to WinterFest and plan all the decorations, music, food, and activities around celebrating the season of winter instead of Christmas.

Inclusion Competencies
Understands how to engage in inclusive behavior (Knowledge):
Understanding ways to include others in roles, processes, and experiences.

Values engaging in inclusive behavior (Value):
Believing that it is important to cultivate a welcoming environment that includes others in roles, processes, and experiences in an effort to encourage a sense of belonging and/or develop a shared commitment.

Has skills to engage in inclusive behavior (Ability):
Being able to include others in roles, processes, and experiences.

Engages in inclusive behavior (Behavior):
Engaging in ways to cultivate a welcoming environment that includes others in roles, processes, and experiences to foster a greater sense of belonging and/or a shared commitment.

Related Competency Areas
- Other Perspectives
- Productive Relationships
- Others' Contributions
- Collaboration
- Diversity
- Others' Circumstances

CAS Domain Translation
- Humanitarianism and Civic Engagement

Leadership Model Translation
- Relational Leadership Model: Inclusive
- Social Change Model: Common Purpose; Controversy with Civility
- Five Practices of Exemplary Leadership: Enable Others to Act
- Emotionally Intelligent Leadership: Capitalizing on Difference

Inclusion Curricular Ideas

Dimension(s)	Curriculum	Other Competency Areas Developed
Knowledge	Have students share examples of inclusive behavior they have seen or experienced. Have them discuss what made these behaviors inclusive.	
Knowledge	Have students share examples of non-inclusive behavior they have seen or experienced. Have them discuss what made these behaviors non-inclusive.	
Value	Have students discuss the advantages for individuals, groups, and organizations of engaging in inclusive behavior.	
Value	Have students research examples of how inclusive leadership has helped a person, group, organization, cause, or community. Have them share these examples.	Research
Ability	Have students analyze a case study and come up with ideas for using inclusive leadership to address the situation.	Analysis
Ability	Have students develop an inclusion plan for an organization they are part of. How could their organization engage in more inclusive behavior?	Plan
Behavior	Have students enact elements of their inclusion plan and report back to the group about the experience in doing so.	
Behavior	Have students intentionally engage in inclusive behavior throughout the week and then journal on what the situation and inclusive behavior were, why they engaged in inclusive behavior, and how that behavior affected the outcome of the situation.	

Social Justice

Leadership exists within a larger social system that often involves an inequitable distribution of social power. Effective leaders have an understanding of social power and the inequities that exist in the distribution of that power, as well as a motivation to lessen or eliminate those inequities. Socially just leaders act in ways that work toward a more equitable distribution of social power and challenge individuals, groups, and systems that reinforce inequity.

Tyler is a junior majoring in business with a minor in sociology. He understands the social power that he has as a male and tries to use that in his day-to-day interactions to make people more aware of sexism, particularly in the workplace. He is quick to confront sexist language and jokes—in his classes, his residence hall, and in his workplace. In some of his sociology classes, he has learned about pay inequities for women. Because this piqued his interest, Tyler applies for a summer undergraduate research assistantship with one of his sociology professors who is studying salary patterns based on sex and gender so that he can better understand pay inequity dynamics, hoping that he can influence positive change in his future in the business world.

Social Justice Competencies
Understands social justice (Knowledge):
Understanding that there is an inequitable distribution of social power within society, resulting in advantages for some and disadvantages for others.

Values social justice (Value):
Believing that it is important to understand that there is an inequitable distribution of social power within society, resulting in advantages for some and disadvantages for others, and that working toward an equitable distribution of social power creates a more fair and just society.

Motivated to act in a socially just manner (Ability):
Being motivated to work toward a more equitable distribution of social power.

Acts in a socially just manner (Behavior):
Working toward a more equitable distribution of social power.

Related Competency Areas
- Systems Thinking
- Power Dynamics
- Creating Change
- Others' Circumstances
- Inclusion
- Social Responsibility

CAS Domain Translation
- Humanitarianism and Civic Engagement

Leadership Model Translation

- Relational Leadership Model: Inclusive
- Social Change Model: Citizenship

Social Justice Curricular Ideas

Dimension(s)	Curriculum	Other Competency Areas Developed
Knowledge	Explain concepts of social power, what it is, how it develops, and who possesses it.	Power Dynamics
Knowledge	Explain concepts of privilege, oppression, equity, and equality and give students examples of each.	
Knowledge	Have students critically analyze the institutions of the media, the education system, government, and others for examples of practices and policies that reinforce inequitable distributions of social power.	Analysis Power Dynamics
Value	Have students research the impact of a social justice effort of a group or organization. What did the group or organization do and how did it contribute to social justice?	Research
Value	Have students engage in social justice simulations that help them understand social power dynamics and how they individually fit into those dynamics.	
Value	Have students interview individuals who have experienced the negative effects of social inequity to learn about how social power dynamics affect individuals.	Others' Circumstances Verbal Communication Listening
Ability	Ask students to share what helps motivate each of them to be a social justice advocate. Have students share experiences of when they acted in a socially just manner and what motivated them to do so.	
Behavior	Have students engage in a social justice project that requires them to select a specific social power inequity and engage in advocacy activities focused on that inequity.	Social Responsibility Advocating for a Point of View

Social Responsibility

Leaders often have the ability to greatly affect others and society through their decisions and actions, whether that effect is positive or negative. Thus, it is vital that leaders engage in responsible decision making and ethical actions so that the impact they leave benefits and does not detract from the welfare of society and its members.

Jill is chair of the annual student carnival, which has been around for thirty-eight years. The carnival is very popular with both students and local community members and often brings in thousands of attendees to go on the rides and play the games. This year, Jill and the planning team were discussing the game prizes at the booths. These prizes have been oversized stuffed animals. After finding that the stuffed animals are made by sources outside the United States with unethical labor practices and that they are nearly immediately disposed of by the winners after the carnival (ending up later in a landfill), the team wants to explore options for more socially responsible prizes. So, the team decides to move away from the stuffed animals and give away prizes like tickets to on-campus theater productions and sporting events, dining coupons, fitness passes, and other items that would be donated by campus departments. Not only do the students like these prizes better, the money that used to be spent on prizes can be donated to a local charity.

Social Responsibility Competencies
Understands social responsibility (Knowledge):
Understanding that one has an obligation to act in ways that benefit, not detract from, the welfare of society and its members.

Values social responsibility (Value):
Believing that it is important to act in ways that benefit, not detract from, the welfare of society and its members in an effort to foster healthy and supportive communities.

Motivated to act socially responsible (Ability):
Being motivated to act in ways that benefit, not detract from, the welfare of society and its members.

Acts socially responsible (Behavior):
Acting in ways that benefit, not detract from, the welfare of society and its members.

Related Competency Areas

- Decision Making
- Helping Others
- Others' Circumstances
- Responsibility for Personal Behavior
- Ethics
- Excellence

CAS Domain Translation

- Humanitarianism and Civic Engagement

Leadership Model Translation

- Relational Leadership Model: Ethical
- Social Change Model: Citizenship
- Emotionally Intelligent Leadership: Citizenship

Social Responsibility Curricular Ideas		
Dimension(s)	**Curriculum**	**Other Competency Areas Developed**
Knowledge	Discuss with students examples of social responsibility. Consider discussing social responsibility in a variety of sectors such as corporations and government as well as individual behaviors that one could engage in to be socially responsible.	
Knowledge	Have students research examples in the news that reflect actions of social responsibility.	Research
Value	Have students discuss the value of social responsibility to a community.	
Ability	Have students share their experiences in being socially responsible. Have them discuss what motivated them to be socially responsible.	
Ability	Have students discuss what motivates people to be socially responsible. Then, have them use this information to develop a plan to motivate others in their lives to be more socially responsible.	Plan
Behavior	Have students discuss with members of an organization they belong to ways that their organization can be more socially responsible.	
Behavior	Have students change one habit or lifestyle behavior to be more socially responsible and report back to discuss with others.	

Service

Serving one's community is essential in creating and maintaining a thriving community. Whether that service is through participation in community processes and decision making, collaborative initiatives, or volunteer positions or experiences, communities are only as strong as their members' commitment and engagement. Leaders model this commitment and engagement to their communities by finding meaningful ways, personally and/or professionally, to participate in service that positively contributes to their communities.

Lars is part of the Education without Boundaries student organization that aims to increase educational opportunities for low-income kids in the community. The organization has been around for eighteen years and has presented a number of events to raise awareness about low access to education. Lars and the other members of the organization have talked a lot about the growing need for tutoring as existing community resources are continuing to be eliminated. The group believes that if their purpose is to increase educational opportunities for low-income students, then they need to serve the community in a much larger way than just offering awareness events. The organization puts together a tutoring program that uses volunteers to help students in a low-income area of town. Lars knows that by serving the community, this program will assist many kids and increase access to educational opportunities for them.

Service Competencies
Understands the value of serving one's community (Knowledge):
Understanding that serving one's community is essential in creating and maintaining a thriving community.

Values serving one's community (Value):
Believing that serving one's community is essential in creating and maintaining a thriving community.

Motivated to serve one's community (Ability):
Being motivated to serve one's community.

Serves one's community (Behavior):
Serving one's community.

Related Competency Areas

- Helping Others
- Social Responsibility

CAS Domain Translation

- Humanitarianism and Civic Engagement

Leadership Model Translation

- Relational Leadership Model: Process-Oriented
- Social Change Model: Citizenship
- Emotionally Intelligent Leadership: Citizenship

Service Curricular Ideas

Dimension(s)	Curriculum	Other Competency Areas Developed
Knowledge	Share with students ways they can serve their community.	
Knowledge	Ask students to identify components of a thriving community. They can brainstorm a list or draw a picture and then share with other students. How might service fit in?	
Value	Ask students to describe an example of a community in which members are not engaged, committed, or involved. What are the impacts of this on the community members?	
Value	Have each student interview someone from an organization or group that has been positively affected by service from others. Have the students share these effects with each other.	Verbal Communication Listening
Ability	Ask students to identify what motivates them the most to serve their community. Ask them to also consider what holds them back from serving their community.	
Ability	Ask students to come up with ways they think would increase others' motivation to engage in serving their community.	
Behavior	Have students engage in service through participation in a community process or decision, a collaborative initiative, or a volunteer position or experience. Then, have them reflect on what they learned about themselves through this experience.	Self-Understanding

Chapter 6
Communication

Verbal Communication

Although the context in which they would need to do it varies greatly, leaders frequently need to be able to communicate effectively with others through spoken word, including oral communication, sign language, and/or communication using assistive technology. This may take the form of speaking in front of a crowd, delivering a presentation, running a meeting, or conversing with someone one on one, among many others. Regardless of its delivery method, effective verbal communication allows a leader to inform, inspire, influence, counsel, and negotiate in a nonwritten format.

The Off Campus Housing Office hosts a housing fair each year that showcases a variety of nearby apartment complexes. The fair has been quite controversial over the years because some apartment complex managers refuse to have their booths anywhere near their competitors', even resulting in verbal altercations on a few occasions. This year, Ethan, the student manager of the Off Campus Housing Office, tells the staff that they will be sitting at the tables this year with certain apartment complex managers. When he hears quite the uproar from his staff about having to "babysit" managers instead of just excluding them from participating, Ethan explains that because these apartment complexes are large university donors, not having them at the fair is not an option. He goes on to share information from his meetings with administrators and student government about the situation and explains all the behind-the-scenes issues so that his staff can understand the full picture. Because he does so, the staff have a better understanding of the situation and are more willing to help.

Verbal Communication Competencies
Understands how to effectively communicate verbally (Knowledge):
Understanding strategies to effectively communicate verbally with others one on one, in groups, and/or in front of a large audience.

Values effectively communicating verbally (Value):

Believing that in order to inform, inspire, influence, counsel, and/or negotiate with others, it is important to effectively communicate verbally.

Has skills to effectively communicate verbally (Ability):

Being able to effectively communicate verbally with others one on one, in groups, and/or in front of a large audience.

Effectively communicates verbally (Behavior):

Effectively communicating verbally with others one on one, in groups, and/or in front of a large audience.

Related Competency Areas

- Appropriate Interaction
- Listening
- Facilitation
- Conflict Negotiation
- Advocating for a Point of View
- Confidence

CAS Domain Translation

- Practical Competence

Leadership Model Translation

- Relational Leadership Model: Process-Oriented
- Emotionally Intelligent Leadership: Influence

Verbal Communication Curricular Ideas

Dimension(s)	Curriculum	Other Competency Areas Developed
Knowledge	Share strategies of effective verbal communication.	
Knowledge	Share pitfalls to effective verbal communication.	
Value	Have students discuss why leaders need to be able to effectively communicate verbally.	
Value	Have students share a time when someone effectively communicated verbally with them. Perhaps they were inspired or influenced or just had their fears calmed by another's words. Have students discuss the impact that the communication had on them.	

Verbal Communication Curricular Ideas

Dimension(s)	Curriculum	Other Competency Areas Developed
Ability	Have students discuss a communication case study in which they need to design an approach for the characters to most effectively communicate with each other to solve their issue.	Analysis
Ability	Have students practice different types of verbal communication: public speaking, one-on-one interactions, running a meeting, or giving a presentation.	
Ability	Have students role-play characters who need to use effective verbal communication strategies to solve a problem.	Problem Solving
Ability	Have each student draw out of a hat a particular communication outcome (inspiration, influence, counseling, negotiation). Have them design and deliver a two-minute speech or presentation with this outcome in mind.	
Behavior	Have students journal about their verbal communication experiences for one week. Have them assess what strategies they used, their effectiveness, and how their communication affected the outcome of the situation.	Evaluation
Behavior	Have students engage in a particular type of verbal communication in a real-life setting: give a presentation to their class, do one-on-one counseling with a peer on an issue, and so on. Have them report back on the experience.	

Nonverbal Communication

Effective communication is more than just communicating words; it is also about body language, gestures, and other cues that convey meaning. Being able to effectively communicate nonverbally allows leaders to fully express their intended meaning and show that they care and they are listening.

As a peer advisor, Tyler often spends time listening to his student advisees as they share their fears and woes of their first semester in college. In meeting with the students, he assures them through his encouraging words that not only are they not alone in their transition to college but that it will get easier. In an effort to completely reassure his students, Tyler makes sure to lean in toward them as they share to demonstrate that he is engaged in the conversation and is concerned, as well as nodding his head a great deal to confirm what they are saying. Tyler finds that because they see the physical demonstration of his support, his students appear to share more with him and trust what he has to say.

Nonverbal Communication Competencies
Understands how to effectively communicate nonverbally (Knowledge):

Understanding ways to effectively convey meaning without the use of words; this may be done through body language, gestures, facial expressions, as well as contact with and proximity to others to either complement verbal communication or serve as communication in and of itself.

Values effectively communicating nonverbally (Value):

Believing that it is important to use body language, gestures, facial expressions, and/or contact with and proximity to others to either complement verbal communication or serve as communication in and of itself in an effort to emphasize and/or convey meaning that may not be able to be solely expressed through the use of words.

Has skills to effectively communicate nonverbally (Ability):

Being able to effectively convey meaning without the use of words; this may be done through body language, gestures, facial expressions, and/or contact with and proximity to others to either complement verbal communication or serve as communication in and of itself.

Effectively communicates nonverbally (Behavior):

Using body language, gestures, facial expressions, and/or contact with and proximity to others to either complement verbal communication or serve as communication in and of itself.

Related Competency Areas

- Appropriate Interaction
- Verbal Communication
- Listening

CAS Domain Translation

- Practical Competence

Leadership Model Translation

- Relational Leadership Model: Process-Oriented
- Emotionally Intelligent Leadership: Influence

Nonverbal Communication Curricular Ideas

Dimension(s)	Curriculum	Other Competency Areas Developed
Knowledge	Brainstorm with students the meaning and use of different gestures and nonverbal communication techniques.	
Knowledge	Have students watch a television show and take note of all the nonverbal behaviors that a particular character engages in. Have them share with others how the character's nonverbal behavior influenced the situation.	
Knowledge	Share with students ways that the norms of different cultures may affect what is deemed appropriate nonverbal communication.	Appropriate Interaction
Value	Have the students discuss the use of nonverbal communication in leadership situations and in what cases it might be most valuable.	
Value	Have students share a time that they experienced someone using nonverbal communication with them that was useful and effective. What was the situation and why was this nonverbal communication useful and effective?	
Ability	Record students in an interaction with others and have them watch to assess their nonverbal behavior, looking for behavior that complemented the interaction as well as behavior that may not have been congruent with the student's intention.	Evaluation
Ability	Have students observe each other engaging in a situation in which they use nonverbal communication. Have the students give each other feedback. Then, have the students implement the feedback through another nonverbal communication situation and be observed again by each other.	Reflection and Application Analysis Evaluation Receiving Feedback Providing Feedback
Behavior	Have students note their nonverbal behavior over the course of one day. What do they find that they do a lot? Is their behavior helpful to the situation? How might their behavior be interpreted?	Evaluation
Behavior	Have students ask for feedback from others about their nonverbal communication. What might others notice that the students themselves do not?	Receiving Feedback

Listening

Effective communication is more than just communicating messages to another person; it also involves receiving messages by listening. Leaders know that effective listening can help prevent miscommunication as well as allow the leader to better understand messages being communicated, gather ideas and feedback, and demonstrate a sense of care about what others want to communicate.

Tanya and Joel are two resident assistants (RAs) who share a large wing in the first-year student residence hall. Each month, they are required to put on a social program that engages their seventy-five students. Usually, they can come up with a program quickly and both agree. But, November's program is creating an issue for them. Tanya wants to plan the program around homecoming and Joel wants to plan it around Thanksgiving. The two of them cannot come to an agreement, and when discussing the issue, they tend to talk over each other and try to argue for their own program idea. Tanya and Joel decide to take a different approach and get to the heart of the matter. They ask each other what it is about their particular program that interests them the most. They agree that while one is sharing, the other will give their complete attention and truly listen. After each has had a chance to share, they decide that doing a program around homecoming is a better option; Joel didn't know that it was the school's hundredth homecoming, and it was sure to be a special event this year. They both agree, though, that a Thanksgiving program is important, perhaps so important that maybe all the RAs in the hall would want to do a building-wide Thanksgiving program.

Listening Competencies
Understands how to listen effectively (Knowledge):
Understanding strategies that assist one in accurately receiving a message that someone conveys through verbal communication.

Values listening effectively (Value):
Believing that it is important to engage in strategies that assist one in accurately receiving a message that someone conveys through verbal communication in an effort to interpret the message as correctly as possible and show care and attention to the communicator.

Has skills to listen effectively (Ability):
Being able to engage in strategies that assist one in accurately receiving a message that someone conveys through verbal communication.

Listens effectively (Skill):
Engaging in strategies that assist one in accurately receiving a message that someone conveys through verbal communication.

Related Competency Areas

- Appropriate Interaction
- Empathy
- Verbal Communication
- Nonverbal Communication

CAS Domain Translation

- Practical Competence

Leadership Model Translation

- Relational Leadership Model: Inclusive; Process-Oriented
- Social Change Model of Leadership: Collaboration; Controversy with Civility
- Five Practices of Exemplary Leadership: Enable Others to Act
- Emotionally Intelligent Leadership: Empathy

Listening Curricular Ideas

Dimension(s)	Curriculum	Other Competency Areas Developed
Knowledge	Share with students techniques for effective listening.	
Value	Have students share a time when they experienced someone truly listening to them. How did it feel and how did having the other person listen to them affect the situation?	
Value	Have students share a time when they didn't listen effectively. What was the situation and what would they do differently next time?	Reflection and Application Evaluation
Ability	Have students pair up and take turns in engaging in effective listening (one verbally communicates and the other listens). Have a third student observe and give feedback to each of the students. Then, have them switch places so that each student will get to serve as the observer once.	Providing Feedback
Behavior	Have students implement techniques for effective listening in a real-life situation. Then, have them reflect on how listening affected the situation and/or the relationship with the communicator.	

Writing

Whether writing out a vision or strategic plan, developing a proposal, writing a performance evaluation of another person, or communicating electronically, leaders need to be able to communicate effectively through writing. Failure to write effectively can result in missed opportunities, miscommunication, or even misrepresentation of oneself or one's organization. Effective writing can help leaders organize ideas, showcase accomplishments, and inspire and influence others, especially when other forms of communication are not an option.

The Campus Information Center is the hub where many students and visitors go for directions, seek answers to questions about the college, and pick up information on college services. The hours of the Campus Information Center are from 8 a.m. to 5 p.m. every day of the week. Students have complained over the years that the Campus Information Center needs to be open later on weekdays because there are more and more night classes offered and thus more student traffic in the evenings. Jared, who is in student government, has heard these complaints from a variety of students and decides that the best way to approach this situation is to draft a proposal about keeping the Campus Information Center open until 7 p.m. on weekdays. He researches campus information centers on other campuses, finds out information about the center's budget, and asks students to write testimonials about the importance of keeping the Campus Information Center open later. He writes the proposal, and, instead of simply complaining about the current hours or just asking that the center be open later, he offers compelling options that showcase ways to extend the hours without increasing the budget. The manager of the Campus Information Center is relieved that this is not a circumstance of another student complaining about the hours. This student, Jared, offers a convincing proposal with thought-out solutions that can be easily implemented.

Writing Competencies

Understands how to write effectively (Knowledge):

Understanding strategies to effectively communicate in a written format, including demonstrating a clear organization of one's thoughts, using words that reflect one's intended meaning, and delivering the information in a readable, clear, and concise manner.

Values writing effectively (Value):

Believing that it is important to communicate effectively in written format to ensure that others accurately and completely understand the message being conveyed through the writing.

Has skills to write effectively (Ability):

Being able to communicate effectively in a written format, including demonstrating a clear organization of one's thoughts, using words that reflect one's intended meaning, and delivering the information in a readable, clear, and concise manner.

Writes effectively (Behavior):

Communicating effectively in written format, including demonstrating a clear organization of one's thoughts, using words that reflect one's intended meaning, and delivering the information in a readable, clear, and concise manner.

Related Competency Areas

- Idea Generation
- Appropriate Interaction
- Advocating for a Point of View

CAS Domain Translation

- Practical Competence

Leadership Model Translation

- Relational Leadership Model: Process-Oriented

Writing Curricular Ideas

Dimension(s)	Curriculum	Other Competency Areas Developed
Knowledge	Share effective writing tips with the students.	
Value	Have students think about a writing piece that was difficult to read because of ineffective writing. What was the piece and how did its writing affect their thoughts about what the piece was trying to achieve?	
Ability	Ask the students to write a one-page paper on a specific topic that is designed to compel the reader to action. Have everyone read each others' papers and give feedback.	Receiving Feedback Providing Feedback
Ability	Have students free-write about a social issue they are passionate about for five minutes. Have them go back and review it for organization, clarity, quality, and articulation of the intended meaning.	Reflection and Application Evaluation
Behavior	Have students engage in writing one of the following: an editorial for the school paper, a proposal about something they want to see changed on campus, a strategic plan for their organization, a grant proposal for a project they are working on, or other topic, utilizing effective writing strategies.	

Facilitation

Groups are powerful engines of problem solving, innovation, and decision making. To best utilize the group process, leaders need to be able to lead discussions effectively, ask the right questions, and synthesize information. Doing this enables groups to maximize their potential in solving challenging problems, generating new ideas, and making difficult decisions.

Chuck and six of his friends have decided to start their own student organization focused on getting incoming students connected to opportunities for involvement. At their first meeting, the group agrees on their values, mission, vision, and even sets their calendar for the year. However, the group is still struggling to come up with a name for their organization. Instead of having everyone argue for their name idea or criticize the suggestions of others, Chuck decides to facilitate the meeting so that the group can productively come to a conclusion about the name. So, Chuck begins by asking everyone to reflect on what images come to mind when thinking of the values of the organization. Then, he tells everyone to write down three ideas for a name and jot down the pros and cons of each. After everyone is done, Chuck gives each person the floor for two minutes to share their ideas. He then asks each person to select their favorite idea, although it cannot be their own, and share with the group what they like about that idea. After the group gets going, Chuck invites the group members, one at a time, to share their opinions and build off of each other's ideas until they come to an idea that everyone likes.

Facilitation Competencies

Understands how to facilitate effectively (Knowledge):

Understanding ways to effectively manage the group process during a meeting, presentation, or gathering without inputting one's opinion by directing the flow of the discussion, asking prompt questions, and keeping the group on track.

Values facilitating effectively (Value):

Believing that it is important to effectively manage the group process during a meeting, presentation, or gathering without inputting one's opinion in an effort to assist the group in reaching the best decisions possible in the most productive and inclusive manner.

Has skills to facilitate effectively (Ability):

Being able to effectively manage the group process during a meeting, presentation, or gathering without inputting one's opinion by directing the flow of the discussion, asking prompt questions, and keeping the group on track.

Facilitates effectively (Behavior):

Effectively managing the group process during a meeting, presentation, or gathering without inputting one's opinion by directing the flow of the discussion, asking prompt questions, and keeping the group on track.

Related Competency Areas

- Synthesis
- Appropriate Interaction
- Group Development
- Inclusion
- Verbal Communication
- Nonverbal Communication
- Listening
- Conflict Negotiation

CAS Domain Translation

- Practical Competence

Leadership Model Translation

- Relational Leadership Model: Process-Oriented
- Social Change Model of Leadership: Collaboration
- Emotionally Intelligent Leadership: Group Savvy; Conflict Management

Facilitation Curricular Ideas		
Dimension(s)	**Curriculum**	**Other Competency Areas Developed**
Knowledge	Share effective facilitation strategies with the students.	
Knowledge	Have students brainstorm characteristics of effective facilitators and characteristics of ineffective facilitators.	
Value	Have students discuss a time in which they experienced ineffective facilitation. What was the situation and how did the facilitation affect the situation?	
Value	Give students a case study and have them discuss how effective facilitation might affect the situation. Then, have them discuss how ineffective facilitation might affect the situation.	Analysis

Facilitation Curricular Ideas (Continued)

Dimension(s)	Curriculum	Other Competency Areas Developed
Ability	Have students share their strengths and challenges as facilitators.	Evaluation Scope of Competence
Ability	Have students engage in a role play in which they practice facilitating a meeting while other students play characters with particular behaviors. Rotate through so that several students have the chance to be the facilitator. Then, have them give each other feedback on the effectiveness of their facilitation.	Receiving Feedback Providing Feedback Verbal Communication
Behavior	If students have the opportunity, have them ask to facilitate a meeting at work, with a group project team, or in an organization they belong to. Ask them to have those in the group they facilitated give them feedback about the effectiveness of their facilitation.	Receiving Feedback Verbal Communication

Conflict Negotiation

Conflict is inevitable. Leaders may be involved in the conflict or helping others negotiate through the conflict. Regardless, conflict happens. Avoiding or mishandling conflict can result in strained relationships, difficulty for people to work together, and issues of trust; it even has the potential to escalate into acts of harm. To create a safe, respectful, and trusting environment, leaders must be adept at negotiating conflict.

As a resident assistant, Josie often hears complaints from her residents about conflicts with their roommates. Some of these conflicts stem from noise issues, having visitors over, or even sharing each other's possessions. Paula and Rosa, two of Josie's residents, have each come to her individually on a number of occasions to complain about the other. Josie has talked with each of them and given them suggestions as to how to interact with each other better. But the conflict has escalated, and Josie needs to meet with both of them to help them work through the conflict. The three of them meet, and Josie leads the meeting off by setting some ground rules for the discussion, like not interrupting or blaming each other. Then, she asks each of them to individually share their experiences and feelings. She is able to take note of all issues that are creating conflict and works with both Paula and Rosa to find common ground, compromise, and even commit to changing their behavior regarding some of the issues. Both residents agree and commit to each other and to Josie that they will work with each other to create a more harmonious living environment for both of them.

Conflict Negotiation Competencies
Understands how to negotiate conflict effectively (Knowledge):
Understanding strategies to effectively manage disagreement, including keeping tension and emotion to a minimum, focusing solely on the issue at hand, balancing the needs and interests of all involved, and finding common ground.

Values negotiating conflict effectively (Value):
Believing that it is important to effectively manage disagreement in an effort to foster a safe, respectful, and trusting environment in which all parties refrain from blame and truly consider each other's perspectives to find common ground.

Has skills to negotiate conflict effectively (Ability):
Being able to effectively manage disagreement, including keeping tension and emotion to a minimum, focusing solely on the issue at hand, balancing the needs and interests of all involved, and finding common ground.

Negotiates conflict effectively (Behavior):
Effectively managing disagreement, including keeping tension and emotion to a minimum, focusing solely on the issue at hand, balancing the needs and interests of all involved, and finding common ground.

Related Competency Areas
- Other Perspectives
- Receiving Feedback
- Appropriate Interaction
- Providing Feedback
- Verbal Communication
- Listening
- Facilitation

CAS Domain Translation
- Practical Competence

Leadership Model Translation
- Relational Leadership Model: Process-Oriented
- Social Change Model of Leadership: Controversy with Civility
- Five Practices of Exemplary Leadership: Enable Others to Act
- Emotionally Intelligent Leadership: Conflict Management

Conflict Negotiation Curricular Ideas

Dimension(s)	Curriculum	Other Competency Areas Developed
Knowledge	Have students take a conflict styles assessment to learn about how they tend to handle conflict.	Self-Understanding
Knowledge	Share with the students effective conflict negotiation strategies.	
Knowledge	Have students share what they do well in terms of negotiating conflict. Then, have students share what is most challenging for them in negotiating conflict. Have students give each other ideas to help them overcome their challenges.	Scope of Competence Receiving Feedback Providing Feedback
Value	Have students discuss experiences in which conflict went unaddressed or was mishandled. What were the ramifications?	
Value	Have students share a time that conflict was handled effectively. What made it effective and what was the impact?	
Ability	Give students a scenario in which two characters are in conflict over a particular issue. Have two students role-play those in conflict and one role-play the conflict mediator. Then, have the students in conflict give feedback to the conflict mediator.	Receiving Feedback Providing Feedback
Ability	Have students watch a film clip in which two characters are in conflict. Stop the clip before any resolution has occurred. Ask the students what conflict negotiation strategies might work best in the situation.	Analysis Evaluation
Behavior	Have students journal after having been involved in a conflict situation about the conflict negotiation strategies they used and their impact on the situation. What might they do again in the future and what might they do differently?	Reflection and Application Evaluation

Advocating for a Point of View

Leaders can have opinions about many issues, causes, situations, and ideas. Leaders may strongly favor one thing and maybe just as strongly not favor another. Effectively communicating what they believe is not easy. So, not only does the communication itself need to be clear and understandable to convey the intended meaning, the leader needs to deliver the information in an influential yet respectful manner. Being able to do this ensures the effective transmission of the message as well as allows the leader to demonstrate a commitment to his or her values, exhibit passion, show others that he or she is willing to put his or her reputation on the line to stand by an opinion, and even convince others to believe what he or she believes.

In their weekly meeting, the Sigma fraternity just decided that for a philanthropy each member will donate $20 to a fund to buy food for the nearby homeless shelter. As good a cause as this is, Rich knows that not all members have $20 to donate and others have much more. He doesn't want to rock the boat because this is such a great philanthropic initiative. Although he has $20 to donate, Rich raises his hand in the meeting and shares that donating $20 may be easier for some than others and that perhaps this philanthropy is optional for individuals. Those who could not afford the $20 were not likely to say anything, so having Rich speak up allowed the fraternity to consider other options.

Advocating for a Point of View Competencies
Understands how to advocate for a point of view effectively (Knowledge):

Understanding strategies to effectively communicate one's beliefs, opinions, or ideas so that others clearly and fully understand both the meaning and significance.

Values advocating for a point of view effectively (Value):

Believing that it is important to effectively communicate one's beliefs, opinions, or ideas in an effort to demonstrate one's passion and commitment and/or influence the opinion of others.

Has skills to advocate for a point of view effectively (Ability):

Being able to effectively communicate one's beliefs, opinions, or ideas so that others clearly and fully understand both the meaning and significance.

Advocates for a point of view effectively (Behavior):

Effectively communicating one's beliefs, opinions, or ideas so that others clearly and fully understand both the meaning and significance.

Related Competency Areas

- Idea Generation
- Decision Making

- Personal Values
- Verbal Communication
- Confidence

CAS Domain Translation

- Practical Competence

Leadership Model Translation

- Relational Leadership Model: Process-Oriented; Purposeful
- Social Change Model of Leadership: Controversy with Civility
- Five Practices of Exemplary Leadership: Inspire a Shared Vision
- Emotionally Intelligent Leadership: Influence

Advocating for a Point of View Curricular Ideas

Dimension(s)	Curriculum	Other Competency Areas Developed
Knowledge	Share with students strategies to advocate for a point of view, such as educating oneself with real examples and data, organizing the argument, and respectful listening.	Listening
Value	Have students read and discuss famous speeches in which people were inspired to action or changed their minds based on the point of view expressed in the speech.	
Value	Have students discuss a time that learning of someone else's point of view changed their minds about something. Have them describe the situation and what it was about that person's delivery that made them change their minds.	Reflection and Application
Ability	Have students research an idea, belief, or opinion that they would like to share with others in a convincing manner. Have them gather as much data and information as possible to develop a well-thought-out presentation.	Research
Ability	Have students write an outline for a one-minute speech expressing their opinion or belief about an issue.	Writing
Ability	Have students prepare a one-minute persuasive speech that showcases their point of view on an issue. Ask the other students to listen and share whether, and to what extent, the speech influenced their opinions on the issue presented.	Verbal Communication Listening

Advocating for a Point of View Curricular Ideas

Dimension(s)	Curriculum	Other Competency Areas Developed
Ability	Have students discuss a controversial topic in small groups. Have them give each other feedback on the presentation of their point of view. What was effective and what could have been improved?	Receiving Feedback Providing Feedback
Behavior	During the course of one day, have students share their opinions about an issue, especially one that may be contrary to what the other person or people in the conversation think. Have them report back to the group about their effectiveness in communicating.	

Chapter 7

Strategic Planning

Mission

Knowing one's values and leading with them is vital to individual and organizational leadership. Because a mission statement is a summary of an individual's or organization's values, it can serve as a decision-making compass that ensures that all decisions are made in alignment with the values. On an organizational level, having a mission statement that reflects the values of the organization and its members can help provide guidance and justification for engaging in particular behaviors and can serve as a binding force for those in the organization who stand behind the values.

The University Service Organization (USO) was created to provide community service opportunities to college students by posting volunteer opportunities of local organizations on the USO website. Last year, Malcolm, an active member of USO, proposed that the group enhance its education efforts and start a reading group as part of the organization. Students would be invited to participate and read books about people serving others and then discuss them. The reading group really took off, so much that now more than half of each meeting and many positions on the board are dedicated to just the reading group. USO leaders bring in local authors to speak to the students, and the entire organization engages in fundraising to buy books for the reading group. The USO is starting to notice that fewer and fewer of their resources and time are going to setting up community service opportunities; they have gathered fewer opportunities for volunteerism, and the website is often not up to date. There is just not enough time to do both the website and the reading group well. So, members of the USO decide that something has to give. The organization does not currently have a mission statement, but the members decide that in order to make this decision and all other major organizational decisions, it is vital for them to lay out their values in a mission statement. After a great deal of discussion, they create the following mission statement: "Connect and serve the community." Through this process they realize that as interesting as the reading group is, it is outside the scope of their mission. So, they scale back the reading group and put more resources into the website, their primary commitment.

Mission Competencies

Understands how to develop a mission statement effectively (Knowledge):

Understanding strategies to develop a mission statement for an individual or organization.

Values developing a mission statement effectively (Value):

Believing that a mission statement is important for an individual or organization as a framework for decision making.

Has skills to develop a mission statement effectively (Ability):

Being able to develop an individual or organizational mission statement.

Develops a mission statement effectively (Behavior):

Developing an individual or organizational mission statement.

Related Competency Areas

- Idea Generation
- Personal Values
- Writing

CAS Domain Translation

- Practical Competence

Leadership Model Translation

- Relational Leadership Model: Purposeful
- Social Change Model of Leadership: Common Purpose
- Five Practices of Exemplary Leadership: Model the Way

Mission Curricular Ideas

Dimension(s)	Curriculum	Other Competency Areas Developed
Knowledge	Have students create a list of their top five values.	Personal Values
Knowledge	Share techniques of developing a mission statement.	
Values	Ask students to share examples of people who consistently demonstrate their values through their actions, so much that others know what their values are without asking.	

Mission Curricular Ideas

Dimension(s)	Curriculum	Other Competency Areas Developed
Value	Have students reflect on a personal value that has guided a decision in their lives. What was the value and how did it affect the decision?	Decision Making Personal Values
Ability	Have students analyze organizational mission statements and try to uncover what the organization's values are simply by reading the mission statement. From what they know from outside the organization, how well do they think the organization is living its mission?	Analysis Evaluation
Ability	Have students develop their personal mission statements and then get feedback from others.	Idea Generation Personal Values Receiving Feedback Providing Feedback Writing
Behavior	Have students work with others in their organization to develop a mission statement if one does not exist.	Idea Generation Writing

Vision

A vision is an aspiration based on what one imagines the possibilities to be in the future; it is a picture of what one wants the future to look like, as an individual, organization, or community. By having a vision in place, a leader can develop goals, plans, and strategies that align with the vision so as to stay on track, keep motivated, and monitor progress toward achieving the vision. In addition, a vision can create a sense of unity between people as they are inspired to achieve the same outcome.

The Emerging Leaders Program is going through an internal evaluation of the effectiveness of the program structure, outreach initiatives, and content. The program staff members have asked several students to be involved in the process. Their first few meetings consist of discussing pros and cons of the current program and developing lists and lists of possible changes. What direction should they go? The group decides to take a step back and create a vision statement for the Emerging Leaders Program. They determine that part of the vision of the program is to involve at least 25 percent of incoming students each year, about three hundred students. Upon coming up with that conclusion, the group is able to drastically narrow down their lists of changes to align with serving a much larger population than they had been. Ideas like arranging for each new student having a one-on-one with the program director

(Continued)

and giving an Emerging Leaders hat to all participants do not seem like viable possibilities, as there just are not enough time and resources to carry out these ideas. In order to keep the essence of those ideas, the group suggests that peer mentors, instead of the program director, offer one-on-ones and awarding an Emerging Leaders pin to students who have completed the program rather than give hats to all participants. By having a vision, the group is able not only to set goals, develop plans, and lay out strategies, but they can also ensure that any decisions they make are consistent with the direction the organization is going.

Vision Competencies

Understands how to develop a vision effectively (Knowledge):
Understanding strategies to develop a statement that defines the aspiration and direction of an individual, organization, or community and how to use it to guide actions and decisions.

Values developing a vision effectively (Value):
Believing that it is important to develop a vision that defines the aspiration and direction of an individual, organization, or community in an effort to create and engage in a long-term strategy to achieve that aspiration.

Has skills to develop a vision effectively (Ability):
Being able to develop a statement that defines the aspiration and direction of an individual, organization, or community to guide actions and decisions.

Develops a vision effectively (Behavior):
Developing a statement that defines the aspiration and direction of an individual, organization, or community to guide actions and decisions.

Related Competency Areas

- Idea Generation
- Writing
- Goals
- Plan

CAS Domain Translation

- Practical Competence

Leadership Model Translation

- Relational Leadership Model: Purposeful
- Social Change Model of Leadership: Common Purpose
- Five Practices of Exemplary Leadership: Inspire a Shared Vision
- Emotionally Intelligent Leadership: Inspiration

Vision Curricular Ideas

Dimension(s)	Curriculum	Other Competency Areas Developed
Knowledge	Share techniques for developing a vision statement.	
Value	Have students interview a member of an organization that has a vision statement and ask how the organization's vision statement affects their work.	Verbal Communication Listening
Value	Have each student research an organization's vision statement—one that has either been achieved or not. Have each student share the vision statement and the organization's progress toward that vision.	Research
Ability	Have students develop their personal vision statements and then get feedback from others.	Receiving Feedback Providing Feedback Writing
Behavior	Have students work with other members of their organization to develop a vision statement if one does not exist.	Collaboration Writing
Behavior	Have students who are in an organization with a vision statement assess how the organization's actions align with the vision statement. What has the organization done to move toward their vision?	Evaluation

Goals

Attempting to achieve a vision can be an overwhelming and daunting task because the vision can be very large and/or take place over a lengthy time span. Thus, it is essential to break the vision down into smaller, measurable, and more readily obtainable goals that contribute to the achievement of the larger vision. By achieving these goals, one can measure progress toward the vision as well as feel a sense of accomplishment along the way.

Sandra's sorority has gotten smaller over the past two years because of a high number of graduating seniors, students transferring to other colleges, and some students leaving the sorority for personal reasons. Because of this, her sorority's focus is on recruiting and retaining a larger membership. At their retreat, the members decide to create a five-year vision of having seventy-five active members of the chapter. Because they have only seventeen right now, that vision seems daunting. So, the members decide to break that down into smaller, achievable goals: twenty-five members by the end of the first year, thirty-five by the end of the second year, fifty by the end of the third year, sixty-five by the end of the fourth year, and seventy-five by the end of the fifth year. By setting these smaller goals, the members have a realistic number to aim for and just enough challenge to motivate but not overwhelm them.

Goals Competencies

Understands how to articulate goals effectively (Knowledge):

Understanding strategies to set goals by laying out targeted measurable objectives that have specified time frames for completion.

Values articulating goals effectively (Value):

Believing that it is important to set goals by laying out targeted measurable objectives that have specified time frames for completion in an effort to give individuals and/or groups small and achievable benchmarks to effectively measure progress and instill a feeling of accomplishment that can continue to provide motivation for achieving an overarching vision.

Has skills to articulate goals effectively (Ability):

Being able to set goals by laying out targeted measurable objectives that have specified time frames for completion.

Articulates goals effectively (Behavior):

Setting goals by laying out targeted measurable objectives that have specified time frames for completion.

Related Competency Areas

- Idea Generation
- Writing
- Vision
- Plan

CAS Domain Translation

- Practical Competence

Leadership Model Translation

- Relational Leadership Model: Purposeful
- Social Change Model of Leadership: Common Purpose
- Five Practices of Exemplary Leadership: Challenge the Process
- Emotionally Intelligent Leadership: Achievement

Goals Curricular Ideas

Dimension(s)	Curriculum	Other Competency Areas Developed
Knowledge	Share strategies for effective goal setting.	
Knowledge Ability	Have students research goals of different organizations and determine whether they are or are not well written in terms of being targeted, measurable objectives with specified time frames. Have students rewrite any that are not well written.	Research Evaluation Writing
Value	Have students share an example of a goal that they set and achieved. Have them share their stories of reaching their goals. What did it feel like? What was the impact?	Reflection and Application
Ability	Have students develop an immediate goal, a short-term goal (one to five years), and a long-term goal (more than five years). Have students share their goals with others and get feedback to ensure that they are targeted, measurable objectives with specified time frames.	Idea Generation Receiving Feedback Providing Feedback Writing
Behavior	Have students review the goals set by an organization they are in to see whether they are targeted, measurable objectives with specified time frames and to what extent progress has been made toward the completion of the goals.	Analysis Evaluation
Behavior	Have students work with their organizations to set goals related to the organizational vision.	Collaboration Writing

Plan

Leaders can be grand thinkers, big dreamers, and aspire to do things no one has ever done. But how do leaders get themselves, others, and their organizations to achieve great things? They must be able to develop a plan to get there. In an effort to reach goals or simply engage in day-to-day organizational operations, leaders must be adept at planning. They must be able to identify tasks and set deadlines so that there is a road map in place to get where the leader, the participants, and the organization want to go.

Jody, Zach, and Angela have been working on a group project for weeks. They must put together a presentation on child literacy in the community. There are many components to this project, and at first the group is quite overwhelmed by the amount of work needing to be done. But, during their first meeting, the group decides that they must lay out a plan to successfully accomplish this project. Jody will work on finding the community resources and writing up descriptions about three agencies in the community that focus on child literacy. Zach will investigate laws in place that may affect child literacy, while Angela does the literature review, looking up research on the issue. They all have their tasks, but to put together the project, they must all complete their tasks by a specified deadline so that they can integrate all the information into the presentation. They plan to complete their parts a week before the presentation is due so that they can come together during that week and complete the presentation. With everyone doing their part, there is no duplication of work, everyone knows what they are doing, they can all contribute to the final project, and most important, achieve the goal of a completing a great presentation.

Plan Competencies
Understands how to develop a plan effectively (Knowledge):
Understanding strategies to lay out a course of action to complete an intended objective by identifying tasks and setting deadlines for completion.

Values developing a plan effectively (Value):
Believing that it is important to lay out a course of action to complete an intended objective by identifying tasks and setting deadlines for completion in an effort to accomplish that objective and work toward a larger goal.

Has skills to develop a plan effectively (Ability):
Being able to lay out a course of action to complete an intended objective by identifying tasks and setting deadlines for completion.

Develops a plan effectively (Behavior):
Laying out a course of action to complete an intended objective by identifying tasks and setting deadlines for completion.

Related Competency Areas
- Idea Generation
- Writing
- Vision
- Goals

CAS Domain Translation

• Practical Competence

Leadership Model Translation

• Relational Leadership Model: Purposeful; Process-Oriented

• Five Practices of Exemplary Leadership: Challenge the Process

• Emotionally Intelligent Leadership: Achievement

Plan Curricular Ideas

Dimension(s)	Curriculum	Other Competency Areas Developed
Knowledge	Share how to develop and use a framework to create a plan.	
Knowledge	Have students look at different strategic plans from particular organizations. Have them identify effective and ineffective aspects of these plans.	Analysis Evaluation
Value	Have students share an example of a plan they have used in their lives. Perhaps it was a one-time plan or maybe it is an ongoing plan. Plans could include how they approach completing their homework, a plan for household chores, or a workout plan. How have these plans helped them achieve their goals?	
Ability	Have students share a plan that they have used recently (homework plan, workout plan, and so on). Have them share with others how their plan assists them in completing their intended goal as well as what they might need to do to enhance the plan. Have them make any adjustments to their plan based on their own reflections or the insight of their peers.	Reflection and Application Evaluation Writing
Behavior	Have students identify one personal short-term goal. Have them develop a plan to achieve this goal.	Writing Goals
Behavior	Have students work with others in their organization to develop a plan around a group goal.	Collaboration Writing

Organization

In addition to the human relations aspect, leadership is often about managing several moving parts such as information, resources, and materials. Leaders need to create systems and structures to most effectively manage, monitor, and utilize these moving parts. Not only does this create ease in navigating structural processes, it allows the leader to spend time on more pressing needs rather than attempting to track down information, resources, and materials.

Robin has been in the Non-Profit Student Association for three years now and during her last year she has offered to be the volunteer coordinator for the largest campus philanthropy event of the year. In her role, she will be coordinating more than a hundred volunteers as well as the materials that those volunteers will need: T-shirts, name tags, and event supplies. Weeks before the event, Robin creates a spreadsheet with all of the volunteer names, their start and end times, their assignments, as well as any event supplies that they need. As the event approaches, she spends time with some of her friends sorting T-shirts into sizes by shift as well as labeling all of the supplies with volunteer names so that she could easily deploy them during the day of the event. This process also frees her up from trying to find certain-sized T-shirts or a particular name tag the day of the event. Instead, she can utilize her time to troubleshoot the check-in process.

Organization Competencies
Understands how to organize effectively (Knowledge):
Understanding ways to create systems and structures that allow one to effectively manage, monitor, and utilize information, resources, and materials.

Values organizing effectively (Value):
Believing that it is important to create systems and structures that allow one to effectively manage, monitor, and utilize information, resources, and materials in an effort to save time, energy, and concern.

Has skills to organize effectively (Ability):
Being able to create systems and structures that allow one to effectively manage, monitor, and utilize information, resources, and materials.

Organizes effectively (Behavior):
Creating systems and structures that allow one to effectively manage, monitor, and utilize information, resources, and materials.

Related Competency Areas
- Systems Thinking
- Plan

CAS Domain Translation
- Practical Competence

Leadership Model Translation

- Relational Leadership Model: Purposeful; Process-Oriented

Organization Curricular Ideas

Dimension(s)	Curriculum	Other Competency Areas Developed
Knowledge	Share ways to organize information, materials, and/or resources.	
Knowledge	Ask students to do a one-minute presentation about how they stay organized.	Verbal Communication
Value	Have students discuss situations in which leaders need to be organized to be effective. Ask them also to think about situations in which being disorganized can have a detrimental impact.	
Value	Have students share a situation or experience in which being organized was helpful. Summarize this information into a list that demonstrates all the ways that being organized has helped the students in the group.	
Ability	Have students research an organization strategy or use one offered by another student to lay out a plan to get and/or stay organized. This may include a plan to buy a day planner and color-code it or create an online filing system for documents. Have students share their plans with each other.	Research Plan
Behavior	Have students enact an organization strategy either personally or in an organization they belong to. Have them report back to the group about the implementation and the outcome.	

Chapter 8

Personal Behavior

Initiative

Leadership often requires action, and a leader is willing to take charge in a situation either individually to fill a need or to help motivate the group to get moving on an idea or task. Leaders do not sit back and wait for someone else to step up; they make things happen. Their contribution may not only fill a need, but can motivate and inspire others to move forward.

There is a big lawn area at the center of campus—the mall—where students gather to relax, play sports, play music, and just hang out. Paula, a junior, often passes the mall on the way to and from class several times a day. Upon closer look, she sees that the mall is almost always covered in trash, which is really concerning for Paula. Paula decides that on her way to and from class, she will carry a trash bag and pick up as much trash as she can. For weeks, she has been able to collect nearly a full bag of trash a day. In the process, other students have seen her do this and have asked her why she is picking up trash. She shares her concerns about all of the garbage and asks each student she talks to whether they would be interested in taking a trash bag with them to and from class to collect trash. By the end of her fifth week of collecting trash, she has mobilized fifteen other students to pick up trash. Not only is this effort removing trash from the area, but now that others notice what a problem the trash is, they have been more conscientious about throwing trash away in a trash bin instead of on the lawn.

Initiative Competencies
Understands the value of taking initiative (Knowledge):
Understanding that it is important to take charge of a situation, voluntarily and unprompted by others, especially when one has the expertise or opportunity to do so or when others are not able to.

Values taking initiative (Value):
Believing that it is important to take charge of a situation, voluntarily and unprompted by others, especially when one has the expertise or opportunity to do so or when others are not able to.

Motivated to take initiative (Ability):

Being motivated to take charge of a situation, voluntarily and unprompted by others, especially when one has the expertise or opportunity to do so or when others are not able to.

Takes initiative (Behavior):

Taking charge of a situation, voluntarily and unprompted by others, especially when one has the expertise or opportunity to do so or when others are not able to.

Related Competency Areas

- Scope of Competence
- Helping Others
- Motivation
- Functioning Independently
- Follow-Through

CAS Domain Translation

- Practical Competence

Leadership Model Translation

- Relational Leadership Model: Empowering
- Social Change Model of Leadership: Commitment
- Five Practices of Exemplary Leadership: Model the Way
- Emotionally Intelligent Leadership: Initiative

Initiative Curricular Ideas

Dimension(s)	Curriculum	Other Competency Areas Developed
Knowledge	Ask students to reflect on what sparks initiative. Why might some people take initiative and others not? Why might some people take initiative in some circumstances but not others?	
Value	Have students discuss a situation in which they didn't take initiative but should have. What might have happened if they had taken initiative in this situation?	
Ability	Have students analyze a case study to determine the expertise and opportunities that make it possible for the characters in the case to take initiative in certain situations.	Analysis

Initiative Curricular Ideas

Dimension(s)	Curriculum	Other Competency Areas Developed
Ability	Have students discuss a time they took initiative, describing what the situation was and what warranted them taking initiative.	
Ability	Have students discuss a situation in which someone else took initiative; why did they take initiative and what did it look like? What was the impact of their initiative?	
Behavior	Put students in a situation in which initiative needs to be taken (a team-building or problem-solving activity). Observe the group to see who takes initiative. Process what caused some to take initiative and others not to.	

Functioning Independently

Being able to function independently is not only beneficial to an individual who is working independently, but it is also advantageous for that individual's supervisor, who may not have the time or interest to provide a lot of oversight, answer a great number of questions, or offer motivation to complete a task. Working independently can assist an individual to develop his or her confidence to complete a task without relying on the input of others, critical thinking skills to seek out answers without having to ask others, and follow-through and motivation by completing a task without being followed up with or reminded.

Katelyn just got selected as an intern for a local nonprofit organization, Kid2Kid Mentoring. Her role is to do a lot of the behind-the-scenes administrative support in setting up and monitoring the mentor relationships between volunteer adults in the community and the fifty kids in the program. Jeannette is the director of the nonprofit and is pulled in many directions trying to do several jobs at once. Kid2Kid is understaffed, and there just is not enough time to get all the work done. So, bringing Katelyn on is quite a relief for the staff. After having been trained by Jeannette, Katelyn knows that she must be able to work independently and not ask for a lot of guidance from the staff because they are so busy. So, she pays great attention to what Jeannette says while training her, so that if she has to clarify a process or ask a question that it will be one that Jeannette hasn't already covered in training. She knows that she needs to be able to demonstrate that she is a self-starter who can be trusted to do her work, do it well, and do it on time with little guidance or supervision. That would be most helpful to the staff, as well as for Katelyn's opportunity to develop her knowledge and skills through this internship experience.

Functioning Independently Competencies
Understands how to effectively function independently (Knowledge):

Understanding how to function without assistance or guidance from others, such as finding answers to questions on one's own and monitoring the progress and timeliness of one's own work.

Values effectively functioning independently (Value):

Believing that it is important to function without assistance or guidance from others, such as finding answers to questions on one's own and monitoring the progress and timeliness of one's own work in an effort to build one's knowledge base and confidence as well as not take time from others' work to assist, answer questions, or follow up.

Has skills to effectively function independently (Ability):

Being able to function without assistance or guidance from others, such as finding answers to questions on one's own and monitoring the progress and timeliness of one's own work.

Effectively functions independently (Behavior):

Functioning without assistance or guidance from others, such as finding answers to questions on one's own and monitoring the progress and timeliness of one's own work.

Related Competency Areas

- Research
- Problem Solving
- Decision Making
- Initiative
- Follow-Through
- Confidence

CAS Domain Translation

- Practical Competence

Leadership Model Translation

- Relational Leadership Model: Process-Oriented
- Social Change Model of Leadership: Congruence
- Five Practices of Exemplary Leadership: Model the Way

Functioning Independently Curricular Ideas

Dimension(s)	Curriculum	Other Competency Areas Developed
Knowledge	Have students discuss what working independently entails and circumstances in which one might need to work independently.	
Knowledge	Brainstorm with students ways to reduce the need to continually ask others questions regarding a task. These may include listening, taking good notes about the task, and making a list of clarifying questions to ask at the onset of the task.	
Value	Have students individually list five reasons why it is important to be able to work independently. Have them share their lists with each other.	
Value	Have the students share a time that they experienced the impact of another person not being able to work independently.	
Ability	Have students share a time in which they worked independently effectively. What strategies did they use to be successful?	
Ability	Have students analyze case studies about situations that arise in which a character may need to work independently. Have them determine the best course of action for each character to be successful at functioning independently in their particular context.	Analysis Evaluation
Ability	Assign each student a task. Without communicating with the other students, have them figure out on their own how to complete the task. Process afterward about the experience and what helped each student in being able to function independently.	
Behavior	Have students journal for one week about all the situations that arise that require them to work independently. What strategies do they use to do this effectively?	Evaluation Writing

Follow-Through

People need to be able to depend on and trust each other to follow through on their commitments even when facing obstacles. An individual persisting through challenge to see something through to the end not only accomplishes the task but also demonstrates that he or she can be relied upon and trusted to carry out commitments.

The Campus Dance Troupe is having their annual car wash to raise money for the spring performance. There are fifty-two students in the organization, and most are responsible for contributing to the car wash supplies. Ryan is in charge of bringing extra towels to dry the cars. On the morning of the car wash (Ryan had to wake up at 6 a.m.), Ryan looks at his clock and thinks that with fifty-one other people helping and him only bringing extra towels, he could just call in sick. But, he knows that if everyone does this, no one will be at the car wash, and it is vital for them to wash as many cars as possible to raise money for the performance. In addition, the group will need the towels he has. So, Ryan pulls himself out of bed, gathers his towels, and heads over to the car wash.

Follow-Through Competencies

Understands the value of following through on responsibilities (Knowledge):

Understanding that it is important to see things through to the end even in the face of adversity.

Values following through on responsibilities (Value):

Believing that it is important to see things through to the end even in the face of adversity in an effort to carry out a commitment to complete a task as well as demonstrate trustworthiness and dependability.

Motivated to follow through on responsibilities (Ability):

Being motivated to see things through to the end even in the face of adversity.

Follows through on responsibilities (Behavior):

Seeing things through to the end even in the face of adversity.

Related Competency Areas

- Motivation
- Organization
- Responsibility for Personal Behavior
- Excellence

CAS Domain Translation

- Practical Competence

Leadership Model Translation

- Relational Leadership Model: Ethical; Process-Oriented
- Social Change Model of Leadership: Commitment
- Five Practices of Exemplary Leadership: Model the Way
- Emotionally Intelligent Leadership: Achievement

Follow-Through Curricular Ideas

Dimension(s)	Curriculum	Other Competency Areas Developed
Knowledge	Ask students to brainstorm all the ways that following through can be beneficial to individuals, groups, and organizations.	
Knowledge	Ask students to think about the impact not following through has on others.	
Value	Ask each person to prepare a one-minute speech that conveys the value of following through. Have them give their speeches to each other in small groups.	Verbal Communication Advocating for a Point of View
Ability	Have students share with others what motivates them to follow through. Is it to conquer a challenge, be seen as reliable, demonstrate one's sense of morality, or something different altogether?	
Behavior	Have students break into groups and give each group a task that they must achieve by the end of one week. After the week is over, bring the students together and ask them to evaluate their own, the group's, and each group member's follow-through.	Evaluation Providing Feedback

Responsibility for Personal Behavior

All people make mistakes and bad choices on occasion. It is how one handles those situations that demonstrates leadership. Leaders do not defer responsibility, push blame on others, or cover up errors. They own up to their actions by admitting when they are wrong, apologizing, rectifying the situation, and accepting the consequences for their actions. Doing this demonstrates a leader's honesty, integrity, and allows the leader to move forward in taking corrective action and learn from the experience so as not to make a mistake or bad choice in this circumstance in the future.

Joey is the treasurer of Hall Council and has to do two office hours per week in the Hall Council office. As a member of the executive board, Joey has been issued a key to the office. Joey notices one day that he seems to have misplaced his office key. At first, he doesn't want to alarm anyone by sharing that it is missing because he is pretty sure that it will turn up. But, after a day of looking, he realizes that regardless of whether it turns up, he needs to take responsibility for losing the key. If he doesn't tell someone, the supplies in the office are not secure. So, he informs his advisor right away and finds out that it will be $100 to rekey the office. Although this is a lot of money, Joey knows that he did the right thing by coming forward.

Responsibility for Personal Behavior Competencies

Understands the value of taking responsibility for one's own behavior (Knowledge):

Understanding the importance of taking responsibility for one's own behavior by admitting mistakes, apologizing, rectifying the situation, and accepting the consequences of one's actions.

Values taking responsibility for one's own behavior (Value):

Believing that it is important to take responsibility for one's own behavior by admitting mistakes, apologizing, rectifying the situation, and accepting the consequences of one's actions in an effort to correct the situation as well as learn from the experience so as to not repeat it in the future.

Motivated to take responsibility for one's own behavior (Ability):

Being motivated to take responsibility for one's own behavior by admitting mistakes, apologizing, rectifying the situation, and accepting the consequences of one's actions.

Takes responsibility for one's own behavior (Behavior):

Taking responsibility for one's own behavior by admitting mistakes, apologizing, rectifying the situation, and accepting the consequences of one's actions.

Related Competency Areas

- Reflection and Application
- Decision Making
- Ethics
- Excellence

CAS Domain Translation

- Practical Competence

Leadership Model Translation

- Relational Leadership Model: Ethical
- Social Change Model of Leadership: Congruence
- Five Practices of Exemplary Leadership: Model the Way
- Emotionally Intelligent Leadership: Authenticity

Responsibility for Personal Behavior Curricular Ideas

Dimension(s)	Curriculum	Other Competency Areas Developed
Knowledge	Have students discuss why taking responsibility is important.	
Value	Have students share a time that someone did not take responsibility for their behaviors. What was the experience, and how did that person's failure to take responsibility affect others?	
Value	Have students share what they believe is the most important reason for someone to take responsibility for their behaviors.	
Ability	Have students write down everything that might hold them back from taking responsibility for a negative action or choice. Have them partner up and share their lists. Have them discuss ways to motivate themselves through these fears and hesitations.	
Behavior	Have students think about an action they engaged in intentionally or unintentionally that had negative consequences. Have them reflect on how they handled the aftermath of the situation. What might they have done differently?	Reflection and Application Evaluation

Ethics

Leaders are not exempt from the standards others are held accountable to; leaders are the model that others follow. Leaders need to be aware that they have been entrusted to make decisions with far-reaching effects and have a responsibility and obligation to hold themselves to a higher standard. Leaders who act ethically can gain the trust of those they work with, inspire others to greatness, and fulfill the duty of care for those they lead.

Aadinath is a student tutor in the learning center. He takes great pride in his writing skills and is often quite helpful for students who need assistance on their Writing 101 papers. Aadinath is working one day, and Mandy, a first-year student in Writing 101, comes in for tutoring for the fourth time for the same paper. Aadinath has worked with Mandy the other three times and is immediately frustrated when he sees her come in again about the same paper. Mandy sits down with Aadinath and starts asking him many of the questions she asked him before and appears frustrated that she cannot finish this paper. It is due tomorrow, and Mandy seems more stressed out than ever. Mandy starts to ask Aadinath questions that would lead him to edit and write the paper for her. Aadinath can tell right away that this could be a slippery slope. Would it be easier for both of them if he helped her reword certain sections? How much guidance should he give before it isn't her work anymore? Aadinath could sense that because of both their frustration levels with this paper that Aadinath could potentially engage in unethical tutoring behavior to alleviate that frustration they are feeling. Knowing that this could be a possibility, Aadinath tells Mandy that he cannot reword sections for her and that she must write the paper on her own. Because he knows that he might not be the best help for her, he offers to find another tutor who hasn't yet seen the paper and can help Mandy with a fresh start.

Ethics Competencies

Understands the value of acting in an ethical manner (Knowledge):

Understanding that ethics are standards of conduct based on socially accepted values and that acting in an ethical manner can promote productive functioning and well-being of groups and society.

Values acting in an ethical manner (Value):

Believing that acting in an ethical manner can promote productive functioning and well-being of groups and society.

Motivated to act in an ethical manner (Ability):

Being motivated to uphold standards of conduct based on socially accepted values.

Acts in an ethical manner (Behavior):

Upholding standards of conduct based on socially accepted values.

Related Competency Areas

- Decision Making
- Responsibility for Personal Behavior
- Excellence

CAS Domain Translation

- Intrapersonal Development

Leadership Model Translation

- Relational Leadership Model: Ethical
- Social Change Model of Leadership: Congruence
- Five Practices of Exemplary Leadership: Model the Way
- Emotionally Intelligent Leadership: Authenticity; Citizenship

Ethics Curricular Ideas

Dimension(s)	Curriculum	Other Competency Areas Developed
Knowledge	Have students discuss scenarios that include unethical behavior. Have them discuss the variety of ways that the unethical behavior in each scenario did affect or could have affected other people or situations.	
Value	Have students brainstorm why ethics are important in leadership. Then, have them discuss what it would be like if most leaders engaged in unethical behavior.	
Ability	Have students reflect on a time that they acted in an ethical manner when it was tempting not to. Have them share what that experience was like and what influenced their decision to be ethical.	
Ability	Have students reflect on a time that they acted in an unethical manner. Have them share what that experience was like and what influenced their decision to be unethical. What was the impact or outcome of their unethical behavior?	
Ability	Have students discuss what makes them and others make unethical decisions. Then, have them think about strategies to reduce their own and others' likelihood to engage in unethical behavior.	
Ability	Have students discuss ethical scenarios and how they would go about addressing them.	Decision Making
Behavior	Have students monitor their behavior over the next week to note ethical dilemmas they encounter. Have them keep track of each dilemma and their decision and/or behavior related to the dilemma. Then, bring the students back together and have them discuss their decisions and/or behaviors in these dilemmas and what course of action they each took. How ethical were their decisions and/or behaviors?	Evaluation Decision Making

Responding to Ambiguity

Because leaders cannot truly control all circumstances and will never know all the answers, they must be able to respond to uncertainty and the unknown. Leaders need to be able to adapt quickly, change direction, and move forward without complete information so they can continue functioning during uncertainty. In addition, embracing that one's plans might get altered or new information might be presented that require a change of course can allow the leader to handle ambiguity with less anxiety, because the only thing that becomes predictable is unpredictability.

Petra is part of LEAD, a leadership workshop program facilitated by student leaders. LEAD just got its start last year and is slow to take off, with weekly workshops often bringing in between three and seven students. The peer facilitators would like to see that number grow, so they blast the campus through social media for their next workshop, one that Petra is facilitating. Because students do not have to RSVP, Petra has no idea how many students will be at her workshop. This affects how much space they will need, how many handouts to make, and even whether the activities will work with a larger group. Petra knows that although she thinks maybe ten students will come, she should probably be prepared for more. Petra looks through the curriculum to find ways to adapt the activities based on group size. She also decides to bring a laptop and projector to show the handout on the screen rather than have to worry about how many handouts to make for an unknown number of participants. Once the students arrive for the workshop, all forty-seven of them, Petra finds a way to situate the room so all the students fit, as well as run all the activities in a way that engages everyone. Although the workshop ends up differently than originally planned, it is still a great success!

Responding to Ambiguity Competencies
Understands how to respond to ambiguity effectively (Knowledge):
Understanding ways to effectively respond to an unpredictable situation, including how to adapt one's plans at the last minute, shift gears as new information is presented, and/or move forward without all the information.

Values responding to ambiguity effectively (Value):
Believing that because nothing is predictable, it is important to be able to adapt one's plans at the last minute, shift gears as new information is presented, and/or move forward without all the information in an effort to both cope and thrive in unknown circumstances.

Has skills to respond to ambiguity effectively (Ability):

Being able to effectively respond to an unpredictable situation, including adapting one's plans at the last minute, shifting gears as new information is presented, and/or moving forward without all the information.

Responds to ambiguity effectively (Behavior):

Responding to an unpredictable situation by adapting one's plans at the last minute, shifting gears as new information is presented, and/or moving forward without all the information.

Related Competency Areas

- Plan
- Responding to Change
- Resiliency
- Positive Attitude

CAS Domain Translation

- Practical Competence

Leadership Model Translation

- Relational Leadership Model: Process-Oriented
- Five Practices of Exemplary Leadership: Challenge the Process
- Emotionally Intelligent Leadership: Flexibility

Responding to Ambiguity Curricular Ideas

Dimension(s)	Curriculum	Other Competency Areas Developed
Knowledge	Share strategies for responding to uncertainty, such as being able to adapt plans at the last minute, shift gears as new information is presented, and/or move forward without complete information.	Responding to Change
Knowledge	Have students read a scenario that presents an ambiguous situation. Have them share as many strategies as they can that might help someone in this situation navigate through the ambiguity.	
Value	Ask students what the impact could be for a leader who does not deal effectively with uncertainty as well as for a leader who does deal effectively with uncertainty. What might be some differences?	

Responding to Ambiguity Curricular Ideas (Continued)

Dimension(s)	Curriculum	Other Competency Areas Developed
Ability	Have students reflect on an experience that was ambiguous. How did they handle it? Then have them share things they do to help them deal with ambiguity.	
Ability	Have students reflect on what might make them anxious about ambiguity. Then, have them identify the skills they need to work on to be able to respond more effectively to ambiguity.	Self-Development
Ability	Give the students a case study that has a great deal of ambiguous information. Have them come up with ways they would respond.	Analysis
Ability	Have students brainstorm a situation that is coming up in their lives that is or has the potential to be ambiguous. Have them think about how they could handle that situation effectively.	Analysis Evaluation
Behavior	For the next time that a student is presented with an ambiguous situation, have them practice utilizing a strategy to respond effectively to ambiguity. Then, have them journal about how they think they handled the situation and whether they would do anything differently.	Reflection and Application Evaluation

Responding to Change

Because of environmental needs, innovation, or matters out of one's own control, change can be sudden, frequent, and stressful. The way a leader responds to change can set the tone for others, affecting both the attitude of the group during the change as well as how successful the transition will be. So, leaders must be flexible and positive but must also be able to adapt quickly so that processes and procedures have a quick and smooth transition and others can move forward and adjust to a new way of being.

Rochelle is the student manager of Freeze, the frozen yogurt food stop on campus. Freeze is a small operation, with only three students and a fairly small budget. Rochelle just learned that all campus food stops will have a 4 percent budget reduction for the following year. Because of this, the director of food services, Rochelle's supervisor, has decided to cut back on staff at Freeze so that instead of having two students working per shift there will be only one. Because demand will continue to be high and staffing lower, a new self-serve yogurt machine will be available so that the student workers do not need to prepare every single serving. This is a big change for Freeze, and Rochelle needs to demonstrate to the other two employees that they can move forward successfully and productively with this change. So, Rochelle first talks with the other two employees to share the positive aspects of this change as well as try to address their concerns so they feel more comfortable with the change. In addition, the three work together to develop new processes so that having one less person on a shift and having a self-service machine is seamless to the customers and becomes ingrained in the culture for the employees of Freeze.

Responding to Change Competencies

Understands how to respond to change effectively (Knowledge):

Understanding strategies that assist one in quickly, positively, and smoothly transitioning oneself and/or others in response to a known or unknown change.

Values responding to change effectively (Value):

Believing that it is important to quickly, positively, and smoothly transition oneself and/or others in response to a known or unknown change in an effort to move oneself, a group, or organization forward productively.

Has skills to respond to change effectively (Ability):

Being able to quickly, positively, and smoothly transition in response to a known or unknown change.

Responds to change effectively (Behavior):

Quickly, positively, and smoothly transitioning in response to a known or unknown change.

Related Competency Areas

- Motivation
- Responding to Ambiguity
- Resiliency
- Positive Attitude

CAS Domain Translation

- Practical Competence

Leadership Model Translation

- Relational Leadership Model: Process-Oriented
- Social Change Model of Leadership: Change
- Emotionally Intelligent Leadership: Flexibility

Responding to Change Curricular Ideas

Dimension(s)	Curriculum	Other Competency Areas Developed
Knowledge	Share strategies to help students respond effectively to change. Focus on how to embed change in one's personal or organizational culture, engaging in adaptability and flexibility, keeping a positive attitude, and assisting others with transition.	Responding to Ambiguity Positive Attitude
Value	Have students discuss a time in which they had to respond to change but that change was drawn out and/or methods to deal with the change were not available. What was that experience like? What could have been done differently to make the transition smoother?	
Ability	Have students review a case study in which a change is being implemented. Have the students brainstorm ideas that the characters could use to effectively respond to the change.	Analysis Idea Generation
Ability	Have students reflect on a time that they had to respond to change. What helped them respond effectively to the change?	
Behavior	Have students utilize strategies to effectively respond to change as they are confronted with changes throughout an entire week. Have them report back about the effectiveness of their use of these strategies.	Evaluation

---

Resiliency

From the perspective of the leader, leadership does not always yield positive results; leaders face challenges and adversity that they cannot overcome, as well as major setbacks and disappointments. But it is the leader who can learn from the experience and rise again to the next challenge who stands out. Many great leaders throughout history have had major setbacks, but we remember them for their ability not only to rise again, but to rise higher than before.

Jake is a first-year student who has been involved in a number of leadership experiences and has solid grades. He is very excited to apply for a resident assistant position for next year because he has been active in his residence hall this year and cannot wait to be on staff. The resident assistant interview process can be intense, and there are often far more applicants than positions. After what Jake thought was a good interview, he finds out that he has not been selected for a resident assistant position. He is angry, hurt, disappointed, and even confused. He decides that the best way for him to deal with his feelings is to find out about his interview performance. After speaking with the staff who interviewed him, Jake gets great feedback and a referral to apply as a Welcome Leader, a residence hall volunteer who helps to transition new students. He decides to apply for that position and is accepted. When resident assistant applications go out again the next year, Jake decides not to apply because he has just been hired as a year-long live-in staff member who oversees all of the first-year transition programs and hall Welcome Leaders, a role that is a perfect fit for him.

Resiliency Competencies
Understands how to demonstrate resiliency (Knowledge):
Understanding ways in which one can bounce back or recover after a setback.

Values demonstrating resiliency (Value):
Believing that it is important to bounce back or recover after a setback, for both one's well-being and success as well as to be better able to face stress, challenges, and adversity in the future.

Has skills to demonstrate resiliency (Ability):
Being able to bounce back or recover after a setback.

Demonstrates resiliency (Behavior):
Bouncing back or recovering after a setback.

Related Competency Areas
- Reflection and Application
- Receiving Feedback
- Responding to Ambiguity
- Responding to Change
- Positive Attitude

CAS Domain Translation
- Practical Competence

Leadership Model Translation

- Relational Leadership Model: Empowering
- Social Change Model of Leadership: Consciousness of Self; Commitment
- Five Practices of Exemplary Leadership: Challenge the Process

Resiliency Curricular Ideas

Dimension(s)	Curriculum	Other Competency Areas Developed
Knowledge	Discuss with students factors that contribute to resiliency and how to engage in resilient behaviors.	
Knowledge	Have students take an online assessment to determine their resiliency levels and what areas they could work on.	Self-Understanding
Value	Have students share a setback they have had and describe what they learned about themselves through that setback. How did that learning affect their future behavior?	Reflection and Application
Value Ability	Have students discuss a time that they demonstrated resilience and what internal attributes helped them be resilient. How was being resilient helpful for them?	
Ability	Have students analyze a current stress, setback, or challenge and then explore how this situation makes them feel. Have them then discuss with another what they can do to be resilient in this situation. For example, if they are feeling out of control, they would discuss what they might do to feel a sense of control in the situation.	Analysis
Ability	Have students brainstorm setbacks in their lives and then list all the positive aspects of how they handled those setbacks.	Positive Attitude
Behavior	Have students journal for a week about all the setbacks they experience and what strategies they used to demonstrate resiliency. Have them report to the group about the experience.	

Positive Attitude

Life is full of unexpected challenges, changes, and actions by others that can be discouraging or defeating. Attitude plays an important role in how one deals with these circumstances. A leader with a positive attitude can foster a sense of optimism, hope, inspiration, and enthusiasm even if the circumstances are bad. Not only are attitudes contagious and having a positive one can help the morale and spirits of others, but being able to find the good in any situation can be empowering and motivating for one's own resiliency.

The Culinary Club just finished competing in a statewide cooking challenge against twelve other clubs from other colleges and universities. The group did a great job and gave 100 percent to the competition. After the competition, each group is notified of who the winning club is. When Wes, the club president, receives a call informing him that the group came in second place, he is disappointed. He knows that he needs to compose himself to be able to share the news with the club with the best attitude possible. He does not want to rile the group up or have them be so upset that they do not participate in future competitions. So, he calls the group together and gives them the news, highlighting what a great job everyone did and how they will work really hard next year to win the competition. He even points out that many members learned new cooking techniques to compete in the event and cooked dishes they have never prepared. He adds that even though they didn't win first place, they had fun and learned a lot. The group seems responsive, and someone reminds them that they did take second place, and that is still better than ten other clubs!

Positive Attitude Competencies
Understands the value of demonstrating a positive attitude (Knowledge):

Understanding the importance of exhibiting an optimistic outlook by identifying the positive aspects of a situation and displaying a "can do" attitude.

Values demonstrating a positive attitude (Value):

Believing that it is important to exhibit an optimistic outlook by identifying the positive aspects of a situation and displaying a "can do" attitude in an effort to foster a sense of hope, inspire oneself and others, and maximize the positive aspects of a situation.

Motivated to demonstrate a positive attitude (Ability):

Being motivated to exhibit an optimistic outlook by identifying the positive aspects of a situation and displaying a "can do" attitude.

Demonstrates a positive attitude (Behavior):

Exhibiting an optimistic outlook by identifying the positive aspects of a situation and displaying a "can do" attitude.

Related Competency Areas

- Motivation
- Resiliency

CAS Domain Translation

- Practical Competence

Leadership Model Translation

- Relational Leadership Model: Purposeful; Empowering
- Five Practices of Exemplary Leadership: Encourage the Heart
- Emotionally Intelligent Leadership: Optimism

Positive Attitude Curricular Ideas

Dimension(s)	Curriculum	Other Competency Areas Developed
Knowledge	Have students discuss how a positive attitude can affect others. Then, have them discuss how a negative attitude can affect others. Why is it important for leaders to demonstrate a positive attitude?	
Value	Have students talk about a time that someone's negative attitude affected them. What did that feel like? What did it do for the situation? Then, have students talk about a time that someone's positive attitude affected them.	
Ability	Ask students to share what motivates them to demonstrate a positive attitude. What strategies do they use to fight off negativity?	
Behavior	Have students take a negative situation in their lives at the time (can be small scale, like a difficult group for an assignment, or large, like a difficult relationship they are in) and write down all the positive aspects of the situation. Have them share these with other students and then discuss how they can maximize those positive aspects in their lives. How does writing this list make them feel?	Reflection and Application Analysis

Confidence

People look to leaders to give them inspiration and assurance. That is why demonstrating confidence is so essential. Followers must be able to believe in their leaders; in turn, leaders must look like they believe in themselves.

Although there are instances in which one may not be confident, demonstrating confidence can help others in their comfort with a situation.

Stephanie and Ray are the student representatives to the Board of Regents. Their role is to inform the board of student issues and advocate for the students regarding institutional policies. The two of them have been called to speak for three minutes to the board in response to a potential tuition increase. Knowing that a lot is at stake, both Ray and Stephanie are nervous. They know, however, that they must appear confident in their knowledge about what students need and want and must be able to show that to the board so that their message is compelling. During their presentation, Ray and Stephanie both demonstrate confidence in what they are saying, so much so that the board invites them back to speak again at the final meeting when the tuition increase vote will take place.

Confidence Competencies
Understands how to demonstrate confidence (Knowledge):
Understanding strategies to appear certain in one's beliefs, knowledge, convictions, and/or capabilities.

Values demonstrating confidence (Value):
Believing that it is important to appear certain of one's beliefs, knowledge, convictions, and/or capabilities in an effort to assure others of one's competence.

Has skills to demonstrate confidence (Ability):
Being able to appear certain of one's beliefs, knowledge, convictions, and/or capabilities.

Demonstrates confidence (Behavior):
Appearing certain of one's beliefs, knowledge, convictions, and/or capabilities.

Related Competency Areas

- Appropriate Interaction
- Motivation
- Advocating for a Point of View
- Resiliency
- Positive Attitude

CAS Domain Translation

- Practical Competence

Leadership Model Translation

- Relational Leadership Model: Empowering
- Five Practices of Exemplary Leadership: Model the Way
- Emotionally Intelligent Leadership: Healthy Self-Esteem

Confidence Curricular Ideas

Dimension(s)	Curriculum	Other Competency Areas Developed
Knowledge	Share strategies related to demonstrating confidence, such as using appropriate body language, verbal cues, and knowing what to do and say in certain situations to appear confident.	Verbal Communication Nonverbal Communication
Value	Have students brainstorm why demonstrating confidence is an important leadership competency. How does a leader who appears confident affect followers?	
Value	Have students share a time that they might not have been confident about something but attempted to appear confident. Why did they try to appear confident? How did that affect the situation?	
Ability	Have students practice communication techniques that help them demonstrate confidence.	Verbal Communication Nonverbal Communication Evaluation
Behavior	Have students identify a situation that they may not feel confident about (going to a social event where they don't know anyone, giving a speech, sharing one's ideals with others, and so on). Have them seek out this type of situation and utilize techniques that make them appear more confident. Then, have them journal about the experience, reflecting on how they felt, what worked, and what the impact was.	Verbal Communication Nonverbal Communication

Excellence

One's ability to lead is a reflection of the work one puts forward. A leader who puts forth the best effort possible, striving for the greatest outcome, can not only accomplish amazing things, but others can look to this person as a model and inspiration to put forth their best effort in all they do.

Jonah works at the library stocking shelves. His peers whom he works with tend to gather together chatting and not moving very quickly to check each bin to see if books need reshelving. But, Jonah takes great pride in his work and moves from bin to bin putting all the books back. He rarely takes a break and sometimes even sets goals for himself for a certain number of books he wants to reshelf during his shift. Jonah's commitment to hard work and his dedicated approach serve as an inspiration to his peers. They see him restocking quickly and getting excited when he meets his goal for the day. They are inspired by Jonah's work, so as a group they set a team goal for the number of books to reshelf in a shift. This helps the productivity of the workers, creates an environment that makes work more fun, and results in a greater availability of books for students to find in the library.

Excellence Competencies

Understands the value of striving for excellence (Knowledge):
Understanding the importance of giving one's best effort.

Values striving for excellence (Value):
Believing that it is important to give one's best effort so as to put forth one's best possible work.

Motivated to strive for excellence (Ability):
Being motivated to give one's best effort.

Strives for excellence (Behavior):
Giving one's best effort.

Related Competency Areas

- Goals
- Initiative
- Follow-Through

CAS Domain Translation

- Practical Competence

Leadership Model Translation

- Relational Leadership Model: Process-Oriented
- Social Change Model of Leadership: Commitment
- Five Practices of Exemplary Leadership: Model the Way
- Emotionally Intelligent Leadership: Achievement

Excellence Curricular Ideas

Dimension(s)	Curriculum	Other Competency Areas Developed
Knowledge	Have students create a list of five reasons why leaders should strive for excellence. Then, have them share their lists with each other.	
Value	Have students partner up and share a time that they gave 100 percent effort to something. What was it and why was it important that they give 100 percent?	
Ability	Have students discuss what motivates them to strive for excellence. What external and internal factors help motivate them?	
Ability	Have students share a time that they were not motivated to give 100 percent. What was the situation and what affected their lack of motivation to strive for excellence? Ask them what they can do in the future to put forth 100 percent in a similar situation.	Reflection and Application
Behavior	Have students break into groups and give each group a challenging task that they have up to a week to complete. After they have completed the task, have them fill out a self-evaluation about the effort they put forth and the contribution they made to the task. Was it reflective of excellence?	Evaluation Collaboration

References and Resources

References

Ammons-Stephens, S., Cole, H. J., Jenkins-Gibbs, K., Riehle, C. F., & Weare, W. H. Jr. (2009). Developing core leadership competencies for the library profession. *Library Leadership & Management, 23*(2), 63–74.

Astin, A. W., Astin, H. S., Boatsman, K. C., Bonous-Hammarth, M., Chambers, T., Goldberg, L. S., . . . & Shellogg, K. M. (1996). *A social change model of leadership development: Guidebook* (Version 3). Los Angeles: University of California, Higher Education Research Institute.

Conger, J. A., & Ready, D. A. (2004, Spring). Rethinking leadership competencies. *Leader to Leader*, 41–47.

Day, P., Dungy, G. J., Fried, J., Komives, S. R., McDonald, W. M., & Salvador, S. (2004). *Learning reconsidered: A campus-wide focus on the student experience.* Washington, DC: The National Association of Student Personnel Administrators and the American College Personnel Association.

Dean, L. (Ed.). (2006). *CAS professional standards for higher education* (6th ed.). Washington, DC: Council for the Advancement of Standards in Higher Education.

Komives, S. R., Lucas, N., & McMahon, T. (1998). *Exploring leadership: For college students who want to make a difference.* San Francisco, CA: Jossey-Bass.

Komives, S. R., Lucas, N., & McMahon, T. (2013). *Exploring leadership: For college students who want to make a difference* (3rd ed.). San Francisco, CA: Jossey-Bass.

Kouzes, J. M., & Posner, B. Z. (2008). *The student leadership challenge: Five practices for exemplary leaders.* San Francisco, CA: Jossey-Bass.

Seemiller, C., & Murray, T. (2013). The common language of leadership. *Journal of Leadership Studies, 7*(1), 33–45.

Shankman, M. L., & Allen, S. J. (2008). *Emotionally intelligent leadership: A guide for college students*. San Francisco, CA: Jossey-Bass.

Resources

Council for Higher Education Accreditation. (2013). *2012–2013 directory of CHEA recognized organizations*. http://www.chea.org/Directories/index.asp

Komives, S. R., & Wagner, W. (2009). *Leadership for a better world: Understanding the Social Change Model of Leadership Development*. San Francisco, CA: Jossey-Bass.

Sharp, M. D., Komives, S. R., & Fincher, J. (2011). Learning outcomes in academic disciplines: Identifying common ground. *Journal of Student Affairs Research and Practice, 48*, 481–504.

CPSIA information can be obtained at www.ICGtesting.com
Printed in the USA
BVOW06s1159040514

352303BV00014B/30/P